GALACTORRHEA

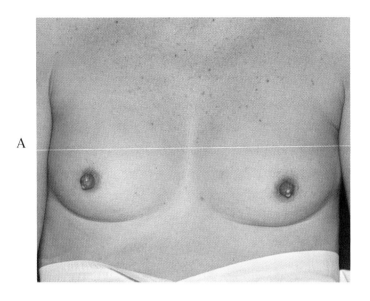

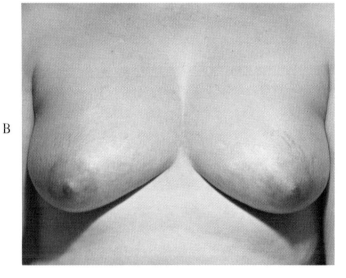

Frontispiece. A) Galactorrhea is usually associated with breasts that appear normal except for the secretion of milky fluid.
B) In some instances of galactorrhea, the breasts may appear full and turgid like the breasts of a pregnant or nursing woman.

GALACTORRHEA

By

BARRY K. GOULD, M.D.

Senior Resident Associate in Endocrinology
Mayo Graduate School of Medicine
University of Minnesota

RAYMOND V. RANDALL, M.D.

Consultant, Division of Endocrinology and Internal Medicine
Mayo Clinic and Mayo Foundation
Professor of Medicine, Mayo Medical School

ROGER D. KEMPERS, M.D.

Consultant, Department of Obstetrics and Gynecology
Mayo Clinic and Mayo Foundation
Associate Professor of Obstetrics and Gynecology
Mayo Medical School

ROBERT J. RYAN, M.D.

Chairman, Department of Endocrine Research
Mayo Clinic and Mayo Foundation
Professor of Medicine, Mayo Medical School
Rochester, Minnesota

CHARLES C THOMAS · PUBLISHER
Springfield · Illinois · U.S.A.

Published and Distributed Throughout the World by
CHARLES C THOMAS • PUBLISHER
BANNERSTONE HOUSE
301-327 East Lawrence Avenue, Springfield, Illinois, U.S.A.

© *1974, by* CHARLES C THOMAS • PUBLISHER
ISBN 0-398-02978-4
Library of Congress Catalog Card Number: 73 12291

Printed in the United States of America

N-1

Library of Congress Cataloging in Publication Data

Main entry under title:
Galactorrhea.

    Bibliography: p.
    1. Lactation disorders. I. Gould, Barry K.
[DNLM: 1. Lactation disorders—Physiopathology.
2. Lactation disorders—Therapy. WP825 G146 1973]
RG861.G34   618.7'1   73-12291
ISBN 0-398-02978-4

PREFACE

TㅎIS MONOGRAPH BEGAN originally as a series of case reports of patients with galactorrhea whom we have seen at the Mayo Clinic in the past several years. We had planned to stress the all too often overlooked fact that patients, who seemingly have idiopathic galactorrhea and amenorrhea or who have what appears to be a sound explanation for their symptoms such as the use of a tranquilizer or birth control pills, often turn out to have an underlying intrasellar or suprasellar tumor.

As we began to correlate our material, a number of exciting new developments took place in the field, generated primarily by a better understanding of the hypothalamico-anterior pituitary relationship and the devising of reliable assays for human prolactin. As a consequence, within the past 18 months there has been a proliferation of information on galactorrhea. These facts, plus the probability that an immunoassay for human prolactin will become widely available within a few months of this writing, prompted us to assemble available current information on galactorrhea as well as our case material into an up-to-date monograph, which we hope will prove timely and useful to those interested in this intriguing subject.

We are indebted to our many colleagues, too numerous to name individually, at the Mayo Clinic who have asked us to see their patients with galactorrhea, to Mr. Payne E. L. Thomas of Charles C Thomas, Publisher, who encouraged us to put our material into monograph form, to Florence L. Schmidt, Section of Publications, Mayo Clinic, who gave us invaluable editorial advice, and to our secretaries, Mrs. Kathleen Welch and Diane C. Halverson, who typed our manuscript innumerable times with skill, patience and understanding.

BARRY K. GOULD
RAYMOND V. RANDALL
ROGER D. KEMPERS
ROBERT J. RYAN

INTRODUCTION

G ALACTORRHEA HAS BEEN DEFINED as "excessive or spontaneous flow of milk" (54). In the accumulated literature, this definition has been altered with the terms "galactorrhea" and "abnormal lactation" being used synonymously.

One of the first written accounts of galactorrhea is found in the Talmud (Sabbath 53B): "It happened with one whose wife died and left a suckling infant and the father had no means to provide for a nurse, then miraculously two nipples like those of a woman have opened from him and so he himself nursed his son." Hippocrates also mentioned a case of lactation in the nonpuerperal breast in "Aphorisms": "If a woman who is not with child, nor has brought forth, have milk, her menses are obstructed" (1).

One of the earliest references to abnormal lactation in the American literature appeared in 1852 when Kneeland (122) described a 35-year-old woman who nursed her child for two years, and after weaning the child, she continued to lactate for an additional three years. Her menstrual periods were regular to the time of conception and after delivery.

The purpose of this monograph is to review some of the pertinent literature on galactorrhea, including its characterization, incidence, classification, pathophysiologic mechanisms and management, and finally to present brief reports and comments on 41 previously unreported cases of galactorrhea.

CONTENTS

GALACTORRHEA

CHAPTER 1

CHARACTERIZATION AND INCIDENCE
OF GALACTORRHEA

B REAST SECRETIONS have been examined in relatively few patients with galactorrhea. Although type and extent of analyses
have differed, the secretions have generally varied from colostrum to normal human milk (25, 39, 67, 113, 130, 144, 181, 184,
217, 242, 245). Secretions show the presence of fat on special
staining. The presence of many white or red blood cells is incom-
patible with the definition of galactorrhea.

Breast biopsy, in patients with galactorrhea, has revealed tissue consistent with that found in involuting breasts after normal
postpartum lactation (130).

Galactorrhea must be distinguished from nipple discharge
from other causes (16). In a series of 1,868 patients who had
breast surgery (128), 152 had previously had a nipple discharge.
Of these 152 patients, only two had milky secretions that the
authors considered to be galactorrhea, which they defined as persistent, nonpuerperal, bilateral, spontaneous nipple discharge
with the color and consistency of skimmed milk. The other 150
patients had grumous, purulent, watery, serous, serosanguineous
or bloody discharges due to ectasia, infection, intraductal papil-
loma, fibrocystic disease or cancer. Grumous discharge secondary
to duct ectasia might be mistaken for galactorrhea, especially in
association with a history of nipple manipulation.

It has been stated that in the absence of the suckling reflex
produced by nursing or other stimulation of the breasts, lactation
usually ceases approximately 14 to 21 days after parturition (96).
In a prospective study that included normally menstruating
parous women between 18 and 44 years of age who were not
taking tranquilizers and who had been pregnant more than 12

months previously, Friedman and Goldfien (70) found breast
secretions in 12 of 48 who were not taking contraceptives and in
11 of 138 who were taking oral contraceptives. Most of these 23
women had secretions from one breast only. Only three patients
were aware of having secretions. In contrast, a group of patients
with amenorrhea-galactorrhea disorders had more copious secretion and about 50 percent had noticed it. Of a group of 114 normally menstruating nulliparous women in the same study, 70 were
taking contraceptives orally but none had breast secretions. Shevach and Spellacy (206) examined 132 parous women, who were
more than a year postpartum and found 42 to have breast secretions; only nine were aware of the secretions. Eight had secretions
from only one breast. Some subjects had secretions at one time and
not at another. Breast secretions were present in 17 of 52 (33 percent) patients using mechanical means of contraception and eight
of 42 (19 percent) patients taking oral contraceptives. None of 29
women who had roentgenograms of the skull had abnormalities
of the sella. Both groups of workers concluded that the use of
contraceptive steroids does not increase the incidence of breast
secretions.

In a study of 3,970 successive, new gynecologic patients in his
clinic, Nyirjesy (165) found amenorrhea-galactorrhea in five
(0.12 percent) and galactorrhea in only 25 (0.63 percent) or a
total of 30 (0.75 percent). Nyirjesy collected 12 additional cases
in which patients had galactorrhea only for a total of 37; etiologic
features were proposed in nine: two had suspected pituitary
adenomas, three had a history of rapid estrogen-progesterone
withdrawal and four were taking oral contraceptives. Except for
those women who were postmenopausal, who had had a hysterectomy or who were taking hormones, all were menstruating.

Pernoll (171) found seven patients with galactorrhea among
9,775 gynecologic outpatients and 318 hospitalized gynecologic
patients seen during one year. Five cases were drug related. One
was associated with autostimulation, and the last, with "anxiety."
All patients with breast secretions were menstruating except one
who had had a hysterectomy.

Of 70 women with pituitary tumors, Ioanitiu *et al* (108)
found 26 with amenorrhea only and 13 with amenorrhea and
galactorrhea.

CHAPTER 2

CLASSIFICATION

THE CONDITIONS ASSOCIATED with galactorrhea are numerous and can be divided into seven categories: (1) Del Castillo syndrome, (2) Chiari-Frommel syndrome, (3) Forbes-Albright syndrome, (4) other disorders and disturbances of the central nervous system (CNS), (5) other endocrine relationships, (6) disturbances of the thoracic wall and (7) drug-related conditions.

The Del Castillo syndrome (Table 2-I) is amenorrhea and

TABLE 2-I.

CHARACTERISTICS OF DEL CASTILLO, CHIARI-FROMMEL AND FORBES-ALBRIGHT SYNDROMES

	Del Castillo	Chiari-Frommel	Forbes-Albright
Amenorrhea	+	+	+
Galactorrhea	+	+	+
Postpartum	0	+	0, +
Pituitary tumor	0	0	+

galactorrhea in a nulliparous female without evidence of a pituitary tumor. It has been called *the syndrome of the lactating virgin.* The Chiari-Frommel syndrome is amenorrhea and galactorrhea occurring postpartum in a female without evidence of a pituitary tumor. The Forbes-Albright syndrome is the occurrence of amenorrhea and galactorrhea in a female with a pituitary (or suprasellar) tumor. There is no consistent relationship to parturition.

Table 2-II presents a more detailed classification of the various conditions associated with galactorrhea and references pertaining to these conditions.

5

TABLE 2-II.

CLASSIFICATION OF CONDITIONS ASSOCIATED WITH GALACTORRHEA
*(With References to Reports in the Literature)**

I. Del Castillo syndrome (cases 1, 2) [3,7,21,25,39,53,55,65,67,71,96,144,166,203,209,217]

II. Chiari-Frommel syndrome (case 3) [2,9,21,25,32,34,35,39,42, 53,55,56,65,75,80,82,86,96, 104,111,114, 132,134,138,145,156,160,175,176,199,203,217,232,236,237]

III. Forbes-Albright syndrome
    A. Chromophobe adenoma (cases 24-29) [32,65,71,72,139,161,190,200,217,223,225,242,244]
    B. Mixed-cell tumor [99,100,106,133,155,170,217]
    C. Basophilic tumor [219]

IV. Other CNS disorders and disturbances
    A. Tumor
        1. Acromegaly (cases 15-17) [14,21,32,46,49,62,66,79,94,105,136,143,188,190,210,232]
        2. Craniopharyngioma (cases 18-20) [5,21,38,90,108]
        3. Pineal tumor (case 21) [32,167]
        4. Other primary tumors (case 22) [93,242]
        5. Metastasis to hypothalamus† [223]
    B. Surgical procedures
        1. Stalk section [57,59]
        2. Resection of intrasellar or suprasellar tumor (case 23)
    C. Sheehan's syndrome [56,67,130,235]
    D. Pseudotumor cerebri [169]
    E. Encephalitis and arachnoiditis [47,177,182]
    F. Tabes dorsalis [56,216]
    G. Syringomyelia [180,189]
    H. Pneumoencephalography [19]
    I. Psychiatric illness [8,30,171]
    J. Pseudocyesis [36,65,203]
    K. Sarcoidosis [66,227]

V. Other endocrine relationships
    A. Primary hypothyroidism
        1. Without sellar enlargement (cases 12, 13) [6,17,21,32,43,58,76,118,186]
        2. With sellar enlargement (case 14) [31,43,100,155,230]
    B. Hyperthyroidism [21,56,65,109,245]
    C. Adrenal carcinoma [23,135,168]
    D. Adrenal cortical hyperplasia [129,203,244]
    E. Chorioepithelioma of testis [41]
    F. Male hypogonadism [233,239]
    G. Hysterectomy [67,77,107,191,204,233]
    H. Ovarian resection [18,77,191,234]
    I. Dilatation and curettage (case 40)
    J. Ectopic tumor production of prolactin
        1. Hypernephroma [220]
        2. Bronchogenic carcinoma† [220]

VI. Disturbances of thoracic wall
    A. Stimulation of male or nonpuerperal female breast [78,83,95,151,162,171,173,204, 231,240]

TABLE 2-II. (Continued)

B. Unilateral mastectomy [11]

C. Mammoplasty (case 30) [95]

D. Thoracic surgery [22,87,181,193]

E. Trauma [22,85]

F. Atopic dermatitis [151,231]

G. Herpes zoster [85]

VII. Conditions related to drugs

    A. Hormones

        1. Estrogen-progesterone combination

            a. During administration [69,84,95,102,171,203,238]

            b. After withdrawal (case 8) [33,69,107,145,185,195,202,238]

        2. Progesterone [26,176]

        3. Androgen (case 10)

    B. Psychotropic drugs

        1. Phenothiazines

            a. Chlorpromazine (Thorazine®, Largactil®) (case 4) [13,40,44,66,103,117,119, 147,159,171,184,212,214,215,218,226,242]

            b. Thioridazine (Mellaril®) (cases 5-7) [103,203,214,242]

            c. Methotrimeprazine, levomepromazine (Levoprome®, Nozinan®) [157]

            d. Trimeprazine (Temaril®) [112]

            e. Piperazine nucleus

                (1) Prochlorperazine (Compazine®) [66,103]

                (2) Thiopropazate (Dartal®, Dartalan®) [157,242]

                (3) Fluphenazine (Prolixin®, Sevinol®) [103,212]

                (4) Perphenazine (Trilafon®) [186,226]

                (5) Thioproperazine, thioperazine (Mayeptil®) [157]

                (6) Trifluoperazine (Stelazine®) (case 7) [103,242]

        2. Tricyclic antidepressants

            a. Imipramine (Tofranil®) [120,214,242]

            b. Amitriptyline (Elavil®, Tryptizol®) [178,242]

        3. Butyrophenones

            a. Haloperidol (Haldol®, Aloperidine®) [186]

            b. Droperidol (Innovar®)† [164,186]

        4. Thiaxanthene derivative—chlorprothixene (Taractan®, Truxal®) [186]

        5. Anti-anxiety drugs

            a. Meprobamate (Equanil®, Miltown®) (case 6) [103]

            b. Chlordiazepoxide (Librium®) [125]

         6. Reserpine (Serpasil®) [13,174,184,208]

    C. Methyldopa (Aldomet®) (case 37) [172,229]

---

*All case numbers refer to present series of cases reported in this monograph in Chapter 12.

†Increased serum prolactin present, but galactorrhea not reported.

CHAPTER 3

PATHOPHYSIOLOGY OF LACTATION

A LTHOUGH CLINICAL observations and laboratory investigations are beginning to clarify the neuroendocrine relationships involved in normal and abnormal lactation, the pathophysiology of specific conditions associated with galactorrhea remains speculative in many instances. No clear explanation can be given for the occurrence of galactorrhea under one set of circumstances and its failure to occur under similar conditions. Even the seemingly *sine qua non* of lactation, a female breast, is not necessary for galactorrhea as evidenced by instances of pathological lactation in males (Table 3-I) .

The mechanisms involved in the growth of the mammary gland and subsequent normal lactation in animals have been studied extensively (53, 141, 153, 211, 242) . Results of hormonal deletion and replacement studies have varied from species to species; therefore the applicability of these observations to man is as yet not entirely clear.

In general, animal experimentation shows that estrogen is responsible for ductal development whereas progesterone is needed for lobuloalveolar growth. In addition, growth hormone (GH) and prolactin have an essential role since, at least in some species, breast development does not take place in their absence. Other hormones seem to be of secondary importance.

After development of the breast, minimal requirements for initiation of lactation appear to be the presence of adequate amounts of prolactin and adrenocorticotropic hormone (ACTH) or adrenal cortical hormones. Insulin is essential for production of lactation *in vitro*. Growth hormone, thyroid-stimulating hormone (TSH), parathyroid hormone and insulin as well as frequent removal of milk from the breasts are necessary to promote maximal secretion of milk. Secretory activity can be maintained by the mammary gland in the absence of removal of milk, but the volume of milk secreted is usually small and not normal in composition (for discussion of the effect of local factors on lactation see Chapter 9). During pregnancy placental factors may substitute for anterior pituitary hormones.

Conditions that initiate the production of milk are not completely understood. A reasonable synthesis of the mechanisms involved is as follows: estrogen acting at the hypothalamic-pituitary level induces prolactin release, possibly by induction of a prolactin-releasing hormone (PRH). High levels of estrogen and progesterone during pregnancy appear to block the release of prolactin from the pituitary and to render mammary tissue unresponsive to lactogenic stimulation. At the end of pregnancy the decrease in both estrogen and progesterone results in lower levels of estrogen, which act at the hypothalamic-pituitary level unopposed by progesterone. In addition, the drop in levels of both hormones leaves the mammary gland receptive to lactogenic stimulation. The role of placental factors, particularly that of human placental lactogen (hPL), in these processes has not been clarified. Since most of the studies supporting these views were done prior to the development of modern assay techniques, future changes in these explanations are to be expected.

Human growth hormone (hGH) and human placental lactogen show many similarities in structure and function to ovine prolactin (oPr), and to human prolactin (hPr) as well, all of which have been shown to possess lactogenic activity. Both hGH and hPL have growth-promoting activity but whether or not prolactin has growth-promoting activity is unsettled and may vary from species to species. Though prolactin has long been recognized as a distinct entity in lower animals, the differentiation of hPr from hGH remained in question until recently. In the past few years extensive studies have demonstrated hPr to be distinct from hGH and several of the physical characteristics of hPr have been determined (20, 28, 66, 68, 72, 92, 101, 106, 108, 137, 170, 183, 187, 203, 209, 211, 242).

Although earlier assay techniques did not demonstrate pro-

TABLE 3-I.
MALES WITH GALACTORRHEA

Author	Associated condition	Comment	Year reported	Age, yr
Oestreich and Slawyk [167]	Psammosarcoma; pineal tumor	Sexual precocity; body growth equal to 7-8 yr; gynecomastia	1899	4
Cooke [44]	Chorioepithelioma of testes	Gynecomastia; secretion — L breast only (colostrumlike fluid)	1915	26
Roth [188]	Acromegaly	Gynecomastia; impotent	1918	28
Bittorf [23]	Adrenal carcinoma with metastasis	Testicular atrophy and impotence; gynecomastia	1919	...
Parkes Weber [108]	Adrenal carcinoma	Gynecomastia	1926	27
Haenel [88]	Angiosarcoma of pituitary	Impotent, 4 yr; lactation, 22 yr	1928	43
Atkinson [10]	Acromegaly	Two males (including Roth's case) in review of 1,319 cases of acromegaly	1932	...
Lisser [135]	Adrenal carcinoma	Gynecomastia; testicular atrophy; watery fluid	1936	33
Staemmler [210]	Acromegaly	...	1940	26
Albores Culebro [4]	Unclassified	Gynecomastia	1946	26
McCullagh et al [150]	Pituitary tumor	Prolactin < normal, ballooning of sella, wt. gain, dull headaches. Radiation and testosterone — no effect. Bilateral mastectomy after 13 yr. Normal sperm; FSH 53-105 mouse units (MU)	1956	26
Russfield et al [190]	Chromophobe adenoma	Gynecomastia; microscopic secretion; FSH 13 MU.	1956	51
Canfield and Bates [32]	Unclassified	Duration 3 mo	1965	24
Wieland et al [239]	Testicular dysfunction	Eunuchoid habitus; gynecomastia for 8 yr. Buccal smear neg; testosterone excretion low; LH and estrogen excretion normal. Penis, prostate, skull, x-ray normal. Testicular biopsy — swollen, vacuolated interstitial cells and maturation arrest of germinal cells. Maternal uncle had similar complaints	1967	18

Author	Category	Description	Year	Case
Chrambach et al (30)	Chromophobe adenoma	Increased plasma prolactin	1971	...
Hwang et al (106)	Unknown	Increased serum prolactin; mild gynecomastia; moderate galactorrhea	1971	...
Finn and Mount (64)	Intrasellar mass	No gynecomastia; galactorrhea for 1½ yr; ceased after radiation to the sella	1971	18
	Enlarged sella	Watery-milky secretion from L nipple for 1 yr. Minimal gynecomastia. Elevated prolactin level. Secretions ceased during radiation to sella		32
Frantz and Kleinberg (68)	Estrogen withdrawal	Elevated plasma prolactin; significant lactogenic activity	1970	...
Forsyth et al (66)	.....	.....	1971	...
Apostolakis et al (242)	Drug induced	Drugs included thioridazine, chlorpromazine, trifluoperazine, haloperidol, and combinations. Galactorrhea in 10 percent of 60 males studied	1972	20 22 23 24
Volpé et al (233)	Testicular dysfunction	Minimal gynecomastia, oligospermia; slight reduction in testosterone and testosterone-production rate; increased serum prolactin. Testicular biopsy showed focal seminiferous tubular atrophy and fibrosis	1972	34 40 27
Gould et al	Metastatic carcinoma	Increased intracranial pressure. On Halotestin 5 mo. X-ray — erosion of floor and dorsum of sella due to metastatic tumor (case 10*)	Present report	30
	Intrasellar mass	Gynecomastia preceded Dx of calcified pituitary tumor by several years. Galactorrhea first noted 3 yr after discovery of tumor (case 11*)		47

*Case numbers refer to present series of cases reported in Chapter 12.

lactin activity in the sera of normal males and nonpregnant females, Hwang *et al* (107) developed an immunoassay sensitive enough to detect prolactin concentrations in the sera of most
humans studied. They demonstrated extremely high prolactin
concentrations in newborn infants, increased concentrations in
20 of 24 patients with galactorrhea of varying etiology, and
normal concentrations in 12 of 13 patients with acromegaly but
without galactorrhea. During pregnancy, concentrations of prolactin increased progressively, then fell to normal levels one to two
weeks after delivery if the mother did not nurse her infant. Suck-
ing was a potent stimulus for release of prolactin, but subsequent
studies showed a progressive decrease in this prolactin response
with increasing time after delivery (74).

Others have demonstrated that patients with galactorrhea of
varying etiology have elevated serum prolactin levels (32, 43, 58,
68, 71, 85, 137, 221, 225, 227, 233, 242), although an occasional
patient with galactorrhea has had a normal or low level (68, 72,
107, 242). Further evidence that prolactin is the final mediator
for abnormal production of milk as it is for normal lactation was
reported by Turkington (223) using an assay employing the rate
of induction of ^{32}P-casein in cultures of mouse mammary gland.
Serum prolactin levels were elevated in a series of patients with
chromophobe adenomas. After attempted surgical removal of the
tumor, those patients who ceased lactating had normal serum
prolactin levels while those who continued to lactate had elevated
levels of prolactin. Similar observations were reported by Nasr
et al (161) in two women with amenorrhea and galactorrhea
associated with a pituitary tumor. Del Pozo *et al* (53) correlated
a decrease in serum prolactin levels with cessation of lactation in a
series of women with postpartum lactation and two others with
galactorrhea.

Friesen (74) has suggested that, in the later stages of normal
nursing and in some cases of galactorrhea in which prolactin levels
are not elevated, it may be that high levels of prolactin are needed
initially to induce lactation but only permissive levels are needed
thereafter.

Other clinical situations in which serum prolactin levels have been shown to be increased include stress such as that caused by surgical procedures, strenuous exercise, sleep and advanced renal failure (74, 146, 164, 194, 242). Although surgery with general anesthesia causes the greater prolactin elevation, proctoscopy and gastroscopy have also been associated with an increase in prolactin. Elevated prolactin has been found in some women who have achieved orgasm with sexual intercourse but not in their male partners. Although local breast stimulation in nonpregnant women may elevate prolactin, the level is not as high as with orgasm (164). Failure of prolactin levels to change during hemodialysis but their tendency to decrease after transplantation suggests that the kidney has a regulatory function on prolactin levels (146).

HYPOTHALAMIC INFLUENCES

It is now firmly established that the secretion of GH, ACTH, TSH, follicle-stimulating hormone (FSH), luteinizing hormone (LH) and prolactin by the anterior lobe of the pituitary and melanocyte-stimulating hormone (MSH) by the intermediate lobe of the nonhuman pituitary is under the control of substances secreted by the hypothalamus. These substances are called *releasing hormones* and *inhibiting hormones.*[1] They are present in minute quantities, seem to be polypeptides and reach the anterior pituitary by way of the long portal vessels that carry blood from the hypothalamus to the anterior pituitary (Fig. 3-1). Three of these hypothalamic hormones have been characterized and synthesized: TSH releasing hormone (TRH) is a tripeptide; LH-releasing hormone (LRH), which also releases FSH, is a decapeptide; and somatotropin-release inhibiting hormone (SRIH) is a tetradecapeptide (29, 60, 148).

While release of the other hormones by the anterior pituitary is under the stimulus of hypothalamic-releasing hormones, secretion of prolactin by the anterior pituitary is thought to be con-

---

[1]Initially, the releasing and inhibiting substances produced by the hypothalamus were called *factors* with the terms *releasing factors* and *inhibiting factors* being used. These substances are now classified as hormones, and hence the terms *releasing hormones* and *inhibiting hormones* are preferred.

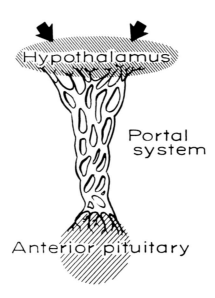

Figure 3-1. Schematic drawing of the long portal blood system. Blood, flowing downward, carries releasing and inhibiting hormones from the hypothalamus to the anterior pituitary.

tinuous and excessive unless held in check by an inhibiting hormone or factor released by the hypothalamus. Experiments in rabbits, dogs and rats in which lesions have been made in specific parts of the hypothalamus, as well as pituitary transplantation experiments, have amply demonstrated the existence of a prolactin-inhibiting hormone (PIH) (50, 89, 97, 98, 115, 149, 154, 163, 197, 205, 211, 213, 243).

Figure 3-2 *left* shows the normal relationship between the hypothalamus and the secretion of tropic hormones and prolactin by the anterior pituitary. If the median eminence, the region of the hypothalamus that secretes the releasing hormones and PIH, is damaged or destroyed, the secretion of tropic hormones by the anterior pituitary decreases while the secretion of prolactin increases (Fig. 3-2 *right*).

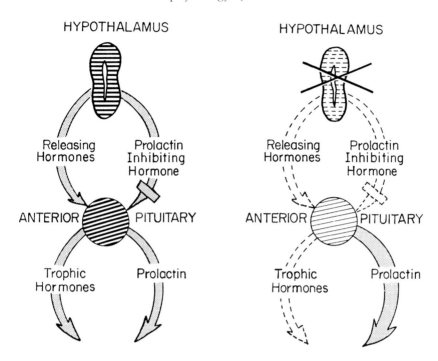

Figure 3-2. *Left,* Normal relationship between the hypothalamus and anterior pituitary. The hypothalamus, by means of releasing hormones, stimulates the anterior pituitary to secrete tropic hormones. Excessive secretion of prolactin by the anterior pituitary is held in check by prolactin-inhibiting hormone produced by the hypothalamus. *Right,* If the hypothalamus is destroyed or the portal blood system is interrupted, hypothalamic hormones cannot reach the anterior pituitary and the production of tropic hormones diminishes while prolactin is released in excessive and uncontrolled amounts.

Evidence for a prolactin-releasing hormone (PRH) has been reported (27, 196, 211, 242). TSH-releasing hormone in pharmacolgic doses has been shown to release prolactin in human beings, but evidence for a physiologic effect on prolactin release is sparse (see Chapter 8). Therefore the exact nature of PRH remains obscure. However, it appears that the secretion of prolactin by the anterior pituitary may be under the control of both an inhibitory and a releasing hormone (Fig. 3-3). Recent studies suggest that a similar dual control by the hypothalamus may be pres-

HYPOTHALAMUS - PITUITARY RELATIONSHIP

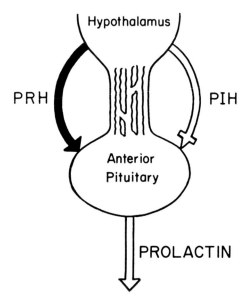

Figure 3-3. Release of prolactin is probably under control of both a prolactin-inhibiting hormone (PIH) and a prolactin-releasing hormone (PRH).

ent for the secretion of MSH and GH by the pituitary. The need for both inhibiting and stimulating hormonal control for prolactin, GH and MSH may be explained by the absence of hormonal feedback from target endocrine glands as is true with the other tropic hormones of the anterior pituitary (196). It would not be unexpected, however, if the secretion of each hormone by the anterior pituitary should ultimately turn out to be the result of interplay between a hypothalamic-releasing hormone and a hypothalamic-inhibiting hormone.

Current thought is that the base-line release of PIH and PRH by the hypothalamus is regulated by a servomechanism or feedback of prolactin itself to receptor sites (as yet unidentified) in the hypothalamus. This feedback loop of prolactin to the hypothalamus is called the *short loop feedback* (Fig. 3-4). It is not

HYPOTHALAMUS - PITUITARY RELATIONSHIP

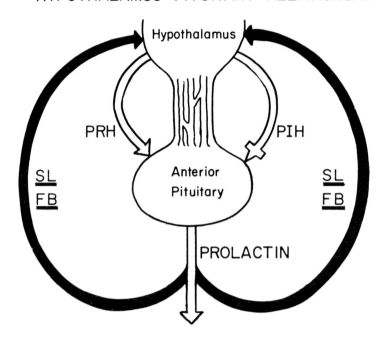

Figure 3-4. *Short-look feedback* (SLFB) of prolactin on unidentified sites in hypothalamus regulates, by servomechanism, the release of prolactin-inhibiting hormone (PIH) and prolactin-releasing hormone (PRH).

known at this time whether PIH and PRH also have an effect on the hypothalamus by an ultrashort feedback loop to play a role in the regulation of the secretion of PIH and PRH (Fig. 3-5).

GALACTORRHEA FOLLOWING PITUITARY STALK SECTION

In the following discussion of galactorrhea associated with pituitary stalk section and pituitary tumors we will omit consideration of PRH and be concerned only with the role of PIH. except as noted.

Clinical experience has shown that interruption of hypothalamic influence on the pituitary can cause increased prolactin

HYPOTHALAMUS - PITUITARY RELATIONSHIP

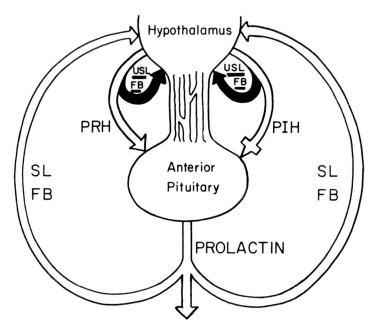

Figure 3-5. It is not clear whether prolactin-inhibiting hormone (PIH) and prolactin-releasing hormone (PRH), by an ultrashort loop feedback (USLFB) to the hypothalamus, play a role in the secretion of PIH and PRH.

secretion (27, 228, 242) and lactation (case 23) (57, 59). When Ehni and Eckles (59) interrupted the hypothalamic-pituitary portal circulation by cutting the pituitary stalk and inserting polyethylene plates in four patients with metastatic mammary carcinoma, lactation ensued. Three patients had previously undergone bilateral oophorectomy, and one of these three had had bilateral adrenalectomy as well, demonstrating that functioning ovaries and adrenals are not prerequisites for galactorrhea. To our knowledge, the only other report documenting galactorrhea developing after pituitary stalk section was that of Dugger *et al* (57), who noted lactation in one of 34 women undergoing this procedure for treatment of metastatic mammary carcinoma.

The explanation for the occurrence of galactorrhea in some patients after pituitary stalk section is that, in some instances, a viable portion of the anterior pituitary remains, usually adjacent to the posterior lobe. This viable tissue, cut off from the influence of the hypothalamic-releasing and inhibiting hormones, fails to produce significant amounts of tropic hormones but does produce, in an uncontrolled manner, large amounts of prolactin. Turkington *et al* (228) have used the term "prolactin secreting organ" to describe this phenomenon of a viable portion of the anterior pituitary lobe producing large amounts of prolactin. As shown in Figure 3-6, PIH does not reach the surviving islet of anterior tissue in significant amounts. If the stalk section is high enough, some of the median eminence of the hypothalamus may

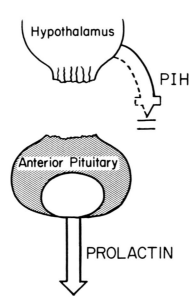

GALACTORRHEA

Figure 3-6. Pituitary stalk section interrupts the long portal blood system and prevents prolactin-inhibiting hormone (PIH) from reaching the anterior pituitary. Interruption of the long portal system usually infarcts most of the anterior pituitary, but a portion may survive (shown in white) and produce prolactin in excessive and uncontrolled amounts.

be damaged and secretion of PIH may decrease or cease. If the hypothalamus is not damaged, theoretically the excessive amount of prolactin circulating in the body should lead, by feedback mechanisms, to increased production of PIH, which does not reach the viable tissue in the anterior pituitary in concentrations sufficient to bring the excessive production of prolactin under control.

PROLACTIN-SECRETING PITUITARY TUMORS

Recent evidence suggests that human pituitary gestation cells are similar in morphology and function to prolactin-producing cells in the anterior pituitaries of other mammals. Such cells normally are found only in women from the third month of pregnancy through the postpartum period and in the newborn during the first days of life (61, 110, 154, 242). The latter observation coincides with elevated prolactin levels and the production of witch's milk in the newborn, though the transplacental effect of maternal hormones may well play an inciting role. Utilizing differential staining techniques, Herlant and co-workers (99, 101, 133) demonstrated the presence of prolactin cells in pituitary adenomas of some women with the amenorrhea-galactorrhea syndrome. According to this group, adenomas described as chromophobic in the past may not have been examined under the proper circumstances to demonstrate a predominance of prolactin cells.

Peake *et al* (170) confirmed the findings of Herlant and co-workers. Histologic study of a pituitary adenoma from a patient with amenorrhea and galactorrhea revealed a predominance of prolactin cells. They found no detectable levels of hGH by immunoassay in plasma after arginine infusion, and extract of the tumor contained only 2 percent of normal cadaver pituitary hGH activity. Pigeon crop assay of the tumor extract showed high lactogenic activity even when the extract was preinoculated with anti-hGH serum.

Hwang *et al* (106) demonstrated lower than normal prolactin activity in the tissue extract of a pituitary adenoma from a woman with amenorrhea and galactorrhea. Prolactin activity in the tumor incubation medium, however, was 30 times greater than normal, demonstrating a high rate of hormone turnover. In another patient with Forbes-Albright syndrome, this group demonstrated elevation of serum prolactin as well as excessive prolactin synthesis *in vitro* by a pituitary tumor (72). Nasr *et al* (161) reported similar findings in their two patients with Forbes-Albright syndrome.

The usual situation in which galactorrhea is found in conjunction with a pituitary tumor is illustrated in Figure 3-7. The tumor itself produces prolactin in an uncontrolled manner. Theoretically, by the feedback mechanism, this should lead to overproduction of PIH, thus shutting off production of prolactin by the normal anterior pituitary tissue.

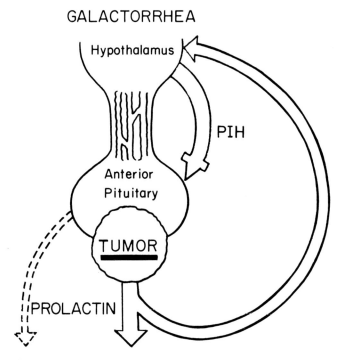

Figure 3-7. Classic situation in which a pituitary tumor produces large amounts of prolactin. Excessive prolactin should stimulate the hypothalamus, by feedback mechanism, to produce large amounts of prolactin-inhibiting hormone (PIH), which inhibits production of prolactin by the anterior pituitary.

Friesen (73, 74) has estimated that 20 percent to 30 percent of "nonfunctioning" pituitary chromophobe adenomas secrete significant amounts of prolactin, thus making this abnormality more common than hypersecretion of GH or ACTH. In his opinion, however, only one-third of these prolactin-secreting tumors are associated with galactorrhea.

OTHER MECHANISMS OF TUMOR-ASSOCIATED GALACTORRHEA

In other hypothetical situations an intrasellar or a suprasellar tumor could lead to overproduction of prolactin and to galactorrhea. A suprasellar tumor could interrupt the portal blood system of the pituitary (Fig. 3-8), thus preventing PIH from reaching

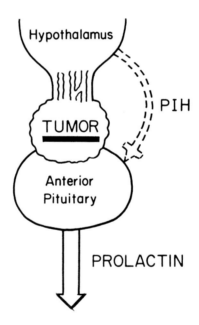

Figure 3-8. A suprasellar tumor may interrupt the long portal blood system and prevent prolactin-inhibiting hormone (PIH) from reaching the anterior pituitary, which would then produce excessive amounts of prolactin.

the anterior pituitary, or the tumor itself could extend into the hypothalamus damaging the cells that produce PIH, thus allowing the anterior pituitary to produce prolactin in an uncontrolled manner. Craniopharyngiomas are most likely to act by these mechanisms, resulting in elevated prolactin levels and galactorrhea.

Theoretically, a pituitary tumor could produce a substance that would act on the anterior pituitary causing it to release prolactin (Fig. 3-9), or the tumor could produce a substance that would block the effect of PIH on the pituitary. Both of these situations should lead to increased release of prolactin by the anterior pituitary and, by feedback to the hypothalamus, to increased production of PIH.

GALACTORRHEA

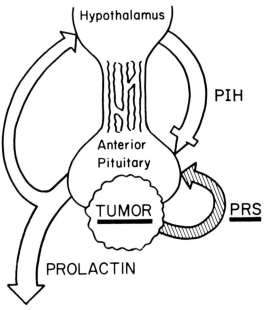

Figure 3-9. Theoretically, a tumor could produce a prolactin-releasing substance (PRS), which would stimulate the anterior pituitary to release prolactin or else block the effect of prolactin-inhibiting hormone (PIH) on the pituitary. Either situation would lead to increased release of both prolactin and PIH.

Figure 3-10 illustrates another hypothetical situation wherein a tumor produces a substance that inhibits the production or release of PIH by the hypothalamus. Uncontrolled release of prolactin by the anterior pituitary would follow.

GALACTORRHEA

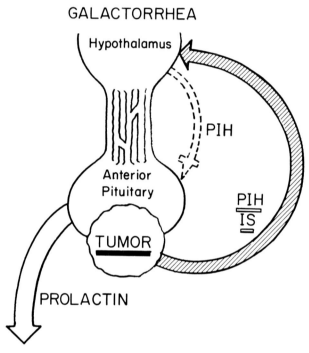

Figure 3-10. Tumor production of prolactin-inhibiting hormone-inhibiting substance (PIH-IS) would theoretically prevent production or secretion of prolactin-inhibiting hormone (PIH). The anterior pituitary would then produce excessive amounts of prolactin.

If one were to invoke the PRH mechanism in addition to PIH (Fig. 3-11), a pituitary tumor could theoretically release a substance that would augment either the production or the release of PRH and would cause the anterior pituitary to produce large amounts of prolactin. Subsequently, by the feedback mechanism, this would lead to increased production of PIH but not in a quantity large enough to prevent excessive release of prolactin by the pituitary.

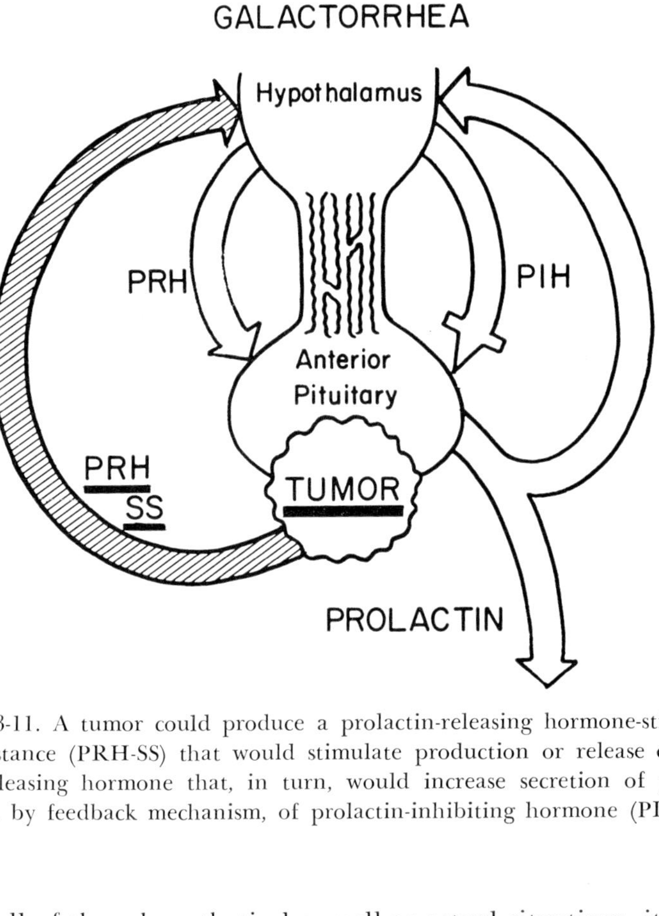

GALACTORRHEA

Figure 3-11. A tumor could produce a prolactin-releasing hormone-stimulating substance (PRH-SS) that would stimulate production or release of prolactin-releasing hormone that, in turn, would increase secretion of prolactin and, by feedback mechanism, of prolactin-inhibiting hormone (PIH).

In all of these hypothetical as well as actual situations, it must be remembered that excess production of prolactin alone does not lead to galactorrhea but, as mentioned earlier, additional factors, as yet unknown, must be present before galactorrhea results.

Since hGH has intrinsic lactogenic activity (242) it is interesting to speculate whether GH or prolactin is responsible for the galactorrhea occasionally associated with acromegaly. Lactogenic activity by bioassay usually has not been elevated in acromegaly without galactorrhea (68, 223). However, Forsyth *et al* (242) have reported the case of a patient with acromegaly, amenorrhea and galactorrhea who had elevated levels of both prolactin and

GH in her serum. To date there have been no further reports of prolactin levels in patients with acromegaly and galactorrhea.

Experimental evidence suggests that hypothalamic catecholamines, particularly dopamine, are transmitters in the hypothalamic release of PIH. Substances that block or prevent dopamine action reduce the output of PIH and hence result in the release of prolactin by the pituitary (see Chapter 10).

The influence of higher centers on the dopamine content of the hypothalamus may explain reported cases in which psychiatric illness is the only evident predisposing factor in patients with galactorrhea (8, 30, 67, 171). In their monograph, Bivin and Klinger (24) compiled 444 cases of pseudocyesis from the literature; 76 gave a history of associated breast secretions. This association of pseudocyesis with galactorrhea is one of the most refined examples of psychosomatic disease.

CHAPTER 4

DEL CASTILLO SYNDROME (AHUMADA-DEL CASTILLO SYNDROME, ARGONZ-DEL CASTILLO SYNDROME)

In 1932, Ahumada and Del Castillo (3) reported the presence of galactorrhea and amenorrhea in an 18-year-old nullipara without evidence of pituitary tumor, with negative urinary gonadotropins and with a small uterus. In 1953, Argonz and Del Castillo (7) reported four additional cases of galactorrhea, amenorrhea and low urinary gonadotropin and estrogen levels with no evidence of pituitary tumor and no preceding pregnancy. Gynecologic examination revealed a small uterus in three of the four patients, but all had normal secondary sexual characteristics. The breasts, including the nipples and areolae, were normal. The amount of galactorrhea varied from the extrusion of a few drops of whitish secretion to the abundant and spontaneous elimination of milk. No history was noted of possible drug induction of galactorrhea or of topical stimulation of the breasts.

Subsequently reported cases have adhered closely to the foregoing description. Women with galactorrhea unrelated to pregnancy and without evident cause are generally amenorrheic and have low levels of gonadotropin and estrogen. Age at onset is usually in the late teens or early 20's. Most patients are nulliparous; many are obese. Breasts are normal as a rule, pelvic examination reveals uterine atrophy and tests of thyroid and adrenal function show normal results. Nyirjesy (166) reported ovarian findings of thickened capsules, atretic follicles, cortical cystic follicles, absence of corpus lutea and marked theca luteinization on ovarian wedge resection in two of his patients, indicating some similarity to the ovaries in the Stein-Leventhal syndrome. This

surgical treatment did not result in any change in his patients'
syndrome. Two patients studied by Lavrič (126) had clinical findings characteristic of the Del Castillo syndrome with polycystic
ovaries on wedge resection. One patient responded with normal
menses and no further galactorrhea.

Rarely patients in the postmenopausal age group have galactorrhea without apparent cause. In such cases the FSH levels have
been in the postmenopausal range (21, 25, 55, 56). Bercovici and
Ehrenfeld (21) postulated that galactorrhea may result in part
from loss of ovarian hormonal inhibition on the pituitary gland.

Cessation of galactorrhea as well as return of menses is rare.
Rankin *et al* (176) stated that spontaneous remission of the Del
Castillo syndrome, such as sometimes takes place with the Chiari-
Frommel syndrome, does not occur. A review of the literature,
in addition to our experience, tends to confirm this belief. Bercovici and Ehrenfeld (21) reported the cases of two patients who
subsequently became pregnant though the mode of treatment was
not mentioned. Haskins and co-workers (96) described a patient
with the Del Castillo syndrome who became pregnant after treatment with clomiphene citrate (Clomid®); after delivery, amenorrhea and galactorrhea returned. Shearman and Turtle (203) reported three cases of secondary amenorrhea and galactorrhea
without apparent cause; the patients ceased lactating and ovulated
after treatment with clomiphene. Treatment with clomiphene resulted in temporary return of menses but increase in galactorrhea
in our case 1. (For further discussion of treatment see Chapters
5 and 11.)

CHAPTER 5

CHIARI - FROMMEL SYNDROME

CHIARI AND ASSOCIATES (35) in 1855 described a symptom complex of persistent lactation, amenorrhea and atrophy of the uterus and ovaries occurring in two young women after delivery. In 1882, Frommel (75), in a report of 28 cases of postpuerperal atrophy of the uterus with amenorrhea, included one case of persistent lactation that fitted the description by Chiari and coworkers. Although Lippard (134) found only 19 cases reported in the literature up to 1961, numerous reports of the Chiari-Frommel syndrome have since been published.

This syndrome is characterized by postpartum amenorrhea and galactorrhea associated with atrophy of the ovaries and uterus without evidence of pituitary tumor. In addition, certain other characteristics are frequently noted. Most patients are primiparous, in the third decade of life, and have a history of oligohypomenorrhea prior to pregnancy. Pregnancy and delivery as well as the early postpartum period are normal. Loss of blood at delivery is not excessive. Association with breast feeding is inconsistent, though the incidence of breast feeding is probably above average. Before the onset of galactorrhea lactation may be greatly decreased or may cease briefly (217, 237). After delivery, menstruation may occur for a few months or years before the onset of amenorrhea (56, 65, 186, 217).

Physical examination usually reveals a slightly overweight to obese young woman with normal appearing or, less commonly, with engorged breasts. Milk may be secreted spontaneously or may appear only with pressure on the breasts. The galactorrhea is usually bilateral. The uterus and ovaries are atrophied, as are the vulva and vagina in occasional cases of long duration. Patients often have a psychic disturbance (case 3).

By definition, the sella turcica must be normal and the visual fields undisturbed. Endometrial biopsy either yields no tissue or atrophied mucosa. Most vaginal smears show a hypoestrogenic condition in contrast to the usual changes observed in the late postpartum period. The morning temperature curve is monophasic, and results of the Fern test are consistently negative. Although urinary gonadotropins and estrogens may be normal, the amounts of both are usually decreased. Withdrawal bleeding may be produced by cyclic estrogen-progesterone therapy. Tests of thyroid and adrenal function show normal results.

Of the classic syndromes associated with amenorrhea and galactorrhea, the Chiari-Frommel syndrome has the best prognosis for at least temporary remission and subsequent pregnancy. Remissions, whether occurring spontaneously or after some form of treatment, are reasonably common. In many cases, pregnancy has followed spontaneous recovery (9, 56, 80, 86, 134, 175, 176, 186, 217). Only in the case of Groseclose (86) and possibly that of Ashkar (9) was spontaneous recovery permanent, however.

Mulla (160) reported a classic example of the Chiari-Frommel syndrome in which the patient was treated by ovarian wedge resection and several drugs, including sodium liothyronine (Cytomel®), betamethasone (Celestone®), acetazolamide (Diamox®), and amitriptyline hydrochloride (Elavil®). Pregnancy and permanent remission ensued. Examination of the ovarian tissue revealed fibrotic thickening of the cortex and numerous follicular cysts producing a polycystic appearance.

Some success has been reported in the treatment of this syndrome with progestational agents. Haskins *et al* (96), using medroxyprogesterone acetate (Provera®), caused cessation of lactation and onset of menses in two patients with Chiari-Frommel syndrome, one of whom subsequently became pregnant. Thompson and Kempers (217) treated one patient successfully with hydroxyprogesterone caproate (Delalutin®); onset of regular menses, minimal lactation and two subsequent pregnancies followed.

Clomiphene has been an agent commonly used for attempting to induce ovulation in patients with Chiari-Frommel syndrome. Rankin *et al* (176) could induce ovulation with clomiphene only in those patients with cytologic estrogen effect. Several successful pregnancies have been reported after one or more courses of this drug (82, 114, 138, 237). Liggins and Ibbertson (132) reported successful multiple pregnancies in a patient with Chiari-Frommel syndrome after treatment with human chorionic and pituitary gonadotropins. Rankin *et al* (176) also noted successes with this combination after failure with clomiphene.

Although successful pregnancies have followed the use of these drugs, a decrease in breast secretions has been effected only occasionally and recurrence of amenorrhea-galactorrhea in the post-partum period is usual.

Recent trials with levodopa (Dopar®, Larodopa®) have produced acute suppression of prolactin in a patient with the Chiari-Frommel syndrome as well as in three patients with Forbes-Albright syndrome and one with postcontraceptive lactation. No effect on lactation was noted (145). Turkington (225) in a more prolonged study demonstrated inhibited secretion of prolactin as well as suppression of lactation in 11 of 14 patients with "idiopathic" amenorrhea and galactorrhea. In this latter study, 0.5 gm of levodopa was given orally every six hours for six months. In five of eight premenopausal women, menses returned to normal. Withdrawal of the drug resulted in recurrence of symptoms and increased prolactin levels. Two patients who responded poorly while taking levodopa were subsequently found to have pituitary tumors. Others have shown similar results (71, 227).

The mechanism of levodopa action is thought to be related to its ability to cross the blood-brain barrier where it serves as a precursor for formation of increased amounts of dopamine in specific hypothalamic centers. Since dopamine is involved in the production of PIH and possibly in stimulating the release of LH-releasing hormone and FSH-releasing hormone, the effects of levodopa can be explained on the basis of increased hypothalamic dopamine levels (225).

In three patients with galactorrhea, Lutterbeck *et al* (140) were successful in decreasing lactation during treatment with 2-Br-alpha-ergocryptine (CB 154), an ergot alkaloid. One woman had evidence of a pituitary tumor, one had postpartum galactorrhea and the third had spontaneous onset of galactorrhea with amenorrhea. Lawrence and Hagen (127) reported disappearance of galactorrhea in four women within three months of institution of oral therapy with ergonovine maleate, 0.2 mg three times daily. Cessation of drug therapy was not associated with return of galactorrhea, and in three women pregnancies occurred—in one after 19 years of amenorrhea. Two of three women successfully nursed and weaned their babies; one was still pregnant at the time of the report. The galactorrhea syndrome did not recur after pregnancy. No other information was given as to the presumed cause of the galactorrhea. Serial serum prolactin levels during treatment with CB 154 were measured in a group of postpartum women and in two women with galactorrhea. Levels of prolactin decreased to normal or immeasurable ranges in all patients and lactation was inhibited. Menses returned in the two women with galactorrhea. One had irregular menses and galactorrhea postpartum (Chiari-Frommel variant) while the other had idiopathic amenorrhea and galactorrhea (Del Castillo syndrome). As opposed to levodopa, which may stimulate hGH and gonadotropin secretion, preliminary screening suggests that CB 154 does not alter the secretion of FSH, LH, GH or ACTH (52).

CHAPTER 6

FORBES - ALBRIGHT SYNDROME

K RESTIN (124), IN 1932, reported two cases of galactorrhea and amenorrhea; one patient was a virgin. Roentgenograms showed evidence of sellar enlargement in both patients but neither had acromegalic features.

In 1954, Forbes and co-workers (65) described 15 nonacromegalic women who had persistent lactation and amenorrhea or irregular menses; all but one had low urinary excretion of FSH. Eight patients had evidence of pituitary tumor with roentgenographic evidence of sellar enlargement; three of these eight had visual field defects and three proved to have chromophobe adenomas on biopsy. The clinical picture was consistent with that of Chiari-Frommel syndrome in four of the remaining seven patients, typical of Del Castillo syndrome in two and associated with pseudocyesis in one. Two of the three patients with features of the Chiari-Frommel syndrome had associated thyrotoxicosis.

Common characteristics among the eight patients with evidence of tumor were as follows: (1) all had had complete amenorrhea for periods of four to 26 years, (2) age at onset of galactorrhea ranged from 16 to 30 years, (3) six were nulliparous, (4) five had hirsutism, four had seborrhea and one had acne and (5) all had low urinary excretion of FSH. A lack of endogenous estrogen was demonstrated by failure to menstruate on withdrawal of progesterone in all five patients in whom this was attempted. Urinary 17-ketosteroids were measured in six patients; in five they were somewhat above average.

Although not all of Forbes' original patients had pituitary tumors, the term *Forbes-Albright syndrome* has come to denote amenorrhea and galactorrhea associated with nonacromegalic pituitary tumor. Chromophobe adenoma has been the tumor most commonly found at operation (cases 24 through 29) (32, 65, 71, 72, 139, 161, 190, 200, 217, 223, 225, 244). One patient, whose case was reported by Thompson and Kempers (217), had an atypical adenoma with a preponderance of eosinophilic cells (mixed tumor) though the patient was not acromegalic. Eosinophilic preponderance has been reported in other cases not associated with acromegaly (105, 106, 133, 170). Toaff and Sadovsky (219) reported the case of a patient who had no clinical evidence of Cushing's syndrome but at operation was found to have a basophilic adenoma. (See discussion of cell type in the section on Prolactin Secreting Pituitary Tumors, Chapter 3.)

Findings reported in subsequently reported cases vary somewhat from those in the original description of Forbes *et al.* Age at onset is usually in the second or third decade. Hirsutism and obesity are not consistent findings. Though amenorrhea is the rule, values for urinary gonadotropins and estrogens vary from normal to low. Tests usually show normal adrenal and thyroid function. Approximately half of the patients are nulliparous.

In several cases postpartum onset of symptoms typical of Chiari-Frommel syndrome with subsequent evidence of intracranial tumor has been reported (cases 17, 18, 20, 21, 25, 26, 27, 31) (21, 32, 37, 39, 65, 81, 91, 108, 130, 133, 139, 140, 158, 198, 219, 244). A lack of simultaneity between the onset of amenorrhea and the onset of galactorrhea is common, with either amenorrhea (cases 29, 30, 35, 36, 38) (21, 32, 63, 161, 170, 217) or galactorrhea (cases 24, 25, 26, 31, 34) (21, 32, 130, 133, 161, 217, 236) appearing first and followed by the other up to seven years later. The three cases reported by Maas (142) and Young *et al* (244) are particularly illustrative, having evolved through both the Del Castillo and Chiari-Frommel syndromes before evidence of a tumor was found (Forbes-Albright syndrome). (See also case 39.)

An association with Cushing's syndrome due to adrenal cortical hyperplasia has been noted (129, 203, 244). Young *et al* (244) reported two cases of intermittent amenorrhea and galactorrhea beginning postpartum. Despite previous roentgenologic evidence of a normal sella turcica, an enlarged sella and symptoms of Cushing's syndrome developed later in both patients. Chromophobe adenomas were found at operation. Turkington (223) reported four cases in which patients with Cushing's disease were treated with bilateral adrenalectomy; chromophobe pituitary adenomas developed subsequently and exhibited evidence of extreme melanocyte-stimulating activity. These women subsequently became pregnant but after delivery had amenorrhea with persistent lactation for two to five years.

Although not classically included in Forbes-Albright syndrome because of their extrasellar position, suprasellar tumors (including craniopharyngiomas, pineal tumors, glioma and astrocytomas) may be associated with amenorrhea and galactorrhea presenting clinically in the same manner as pituitary adenomas (cases 18 through 22) (5, 21, 32, 38, 90, 108, 167, 242). (See the section on Other Mechanisms of Tumor-Associated Galactorrhea, Chapter 3.)

The patient's future well-being is dependent on the natural history of the tumor as well as the results of treatment. No form of therapy has been consistently successful in alleviating the amenorrhea and galactorrhea of these patients. (See Chapters 5 and 11.)

CHAPTER 7

OTHER CENTRAL NERVOUS SYSTEM DISORDERS ASSOCIATED WITH GALACTORRHEA

ACROMEGALY

IN THE LITERATURE, acromegaly has not been included under the classification of Forbes-Albright syndrome because of its previously recognized association with galactorrhea. Galactorrhea in a female acromegalic was recognized late in the 19th century (62). Roth (188) reported occurrence of galactorrhea in a male acromegalic in 1918. Davidoff (49) noted galactorrhea in four of 56 female acromegalics. Of 100 cases of acromegaly reviewed by Gordon *et al* (79), two of 52 females had abnormal lactation. Of 17 women in a series of 30 acromegalics reported by Hamwi *et al* (94) only one had galactorrhea and this developed after radiation to the sella. Others have also noted the association of acromegaly and galactorrhea (Table 7-I). The classic features of the acromegalic state are present and the sella is usually enlarged. Associated amenorrhea is the rule. In several patients, the onset of galactorrhea has followed delivery (case 17) (14, 46, 49, 105, 232). In general, reports have not included extensive descriptions or laboratory data; therefore a more detailed characterization is not yet possible. No case of pregnancy after the onset of galactorrhea has been described previously in patients with acromegaly. However, one of us (R.J.R.) did see an acromegalic woman who had had amenorrhea and galactorrhea for six years. She was given radiation therapy and for the next four years she received norethynodrel with mestranol (Enovid®). After the medication was discontinued she became pregnant and had a normal delivery.

SHEEHAN'S SYNDROME

Cases of anterior pituitary failure in the postpartum period associated with galactorrhea are described in several papers (56, 67, 130, 235). In no case was there evidence of pituitary tumor. In all cases, save that of Foss and Short (67), severe postpartum hemorrhage was reported. In the case reported by Dowling *et al* (56) the patient ceased lactating and resumed irregular menses while receiving cortisone and thyroid replacement. She later became pregnant and delivered a full-term infant. The patient of Levine *et al* (130) ceased lactating and resumed menstruating while receiving similar therapy. She became pregnant, but aborted spontaneously. In the case reported by Wanebo and Rawson (235) the patient also had Hodgkin's disease, rheumatoid arthritis and lupus erythematosus and had had an episode of acute thyroiditis. Galactorrhea ceased and menses resumed spontaneously four years after delivery.

SARCOIDOSIS

Recently Turkington and MacIndoe (227) have reported the occurrence of hyperprolactinemia in sarcoidosis. Of 34 patients with extrapulmonary sarcoidosis (ten men, 24 women), eleven (three men, eight women) had elevated serum prolactin levels. Four women with elevated serum prolactin levels had amenorrhea and galactorrhea and were treated with levodopa for two months. Three responded with cessation of galactorrhea, increased gonadotropin secretion and resumption of menses. On the basis of autopsy findings in one male patient and the absence of associated endocrine abnormalities in six patients, the authors suggested that sarcoid granulomas may selectively destroy specific hypothalamic nuclei that normally inhibit the secretion of prolactin by the anterior pituitary. They further suggested the possibility that hypothalamic sarcoidosis might have etiologic significance in cases of idiopathic galactorrhea-amenorrhea syndromes (Chiari-Frommel, Del Castillo). The association of cerebral sarcoidosis with galactorrhea has also been noted by Forsyth *et al* (66).

Galactorrhea has been associated with various disturbances of the central nervous system which may or may not have affected

TABLE 7-I.
GALACTORRHEA ASSOCIATED WITH ACROMEGALY

Author	Gravida/Para	Menses	Comment	Year reported	Age, yr
Fazio [62]	...	...	Duration — 4 yr; onset after pregnancy and weaning	1896	...
Maguire [143]	...	Amenorrhea	Duration — 3 yr; menopause 3 yr earlier	1909	...
Lodge [130]	...	Amenorrhea		1912	27
Bab [14]	...	...	Recent pregnancy	1914	...
Roth [188]	...	...	Male. Impotent; gynecomastia	1918	28
Davidoff [49]	...	...	4 of 56 female acromegalics; unilateral in 3, bilateral in 1	1926	...
	...	Amenorrhea	Case not in above series. Duration — 5 yr; onset postpartum. Acromegaly discovered after 5 yr	1926	...
Atkinson [10]	.....	.....	In review of 1,319 cases of acromegaly including the foregoing series; 7 had galactorrhea (2 males)	1932	...
Cushing [40]	...	Amenorrhea	Onset postpartum; wt. gain; irradiation decreased lactation but amenorrhea persisted	1933	...
Del Castillo and Lanari [51]	G-0	...	...	1933	...
Staemmler [210]	...	...	Male	1940	26
Hurxthal et al [105]	...	Amenorrhea	Onset postpartum; radiation — no effect on lactation; stilbestrol — temporary relief	1949	32
Russfield et al [190]	G-0	Amenorrhea	FSH 7 mouse units (MU)	1956	25
Hamwi et al [90]	...	Amenorrhea	Galactorrhea after radiation to sella; 1 of 30 patients (17 women)	1960	...

Vix [202]	...	Amenorrhea	Duration — 5 yr; onset post partum; stilbestrol suppressed lactation; radiation arrested growth of tumor	1961	25
Gordon et al [70]	...	...	100 acromegalics (48 males, 52 females); 2 females — transient galactorrhea disclosed only by direct questioning	1962	...
Bercovici and Ehrenfeld [21]	...	...	3 cases mentioned	1963	...
Canfield and Bates [32]	G-0	Normal	Duration — 4 yr. Urinary FSH >5<50. 17-hydroxycorticosteroids 3.7 mg/24 hr. 17-ketosteroids 7.3 mg/24 hr	1965	30
Forsyth et al [60]	...	Amenorrhea	Increased lactogenic activity in plasma not crossreacting with hGH	1971	20
Gould et al	4/3/1	Amenorrhea	Onset post partum (case 15*)	Present report	33
	6/4/2	Irregular	Onset ? post partum (case 16*)		42
	3/3	Amenorrhea	Radiation to sella; secretions ceased (case 17*)		35

*Case numbers refer to present series of cases reported in Chapter 12.

the hypothalamic-pituitary axis directly. These include encephalitis, arachnoiditis, tabes dorsalis, pseudotumor cerebri, syringomyelia and pneumoencephalography (Table 2-II). Extensive studies were not done in these patients and the pathophysiology remains obscure.

CHAPTER 8

OTHER ENDOCRINE DISORDERS ASSOCIATED WITH GALACTORRHEA

D ISORDERS OF OTHER endocrine glands have been associated with galactorrhea (Table 2-II), but the mechanisms involved have not been well delineated.

Van Wyk and Grumbach (230) described a syndrome of precocious menstruation and galactorrhea with juvenile hypothyroidism in three girls. The association of hypothyroidism with various manifestations of sexual precocity, including galactorrhea, and reversion to a prepubescent state after the institution of therapy with thyroid were the essential findings. Failure of the thyroid was primary, with no response to administration of TSH. Visual field defects were absent, but roentgenograms showed evidence of enlarged sellas. The sellas returned to normal size after treatment with desiccated thyroid. The authors postulated a hormonal overlap with increased production of other anterior pituitary hormones related to increased production of TSH. Chromophobe adenoma could not be ruled out, but the more probable etiology was thought to be hyperplasia of the anterior pituitary since the process was reversible. (See also case 14.)

In four patients with primary hypothyroidism but otherwise characteristic of Chiari-Frommel syndrome, Kinch *et al* (118) postulated that the primary hypothyroidism may have caused a metabolic depression of hypothalamic gonadotropin-releasing factors as well as prolactin-inhibiting factor due to selective overproduction of TSH. Others have reported similar cases of primary myxedema with galactorrhea usually occurring after delivery and associated with amenorrhea. Sellas were normal. Thyroid replacement has been almost uniformly successful in stopping lactation.

41

Subsequent pregnancies have occurred in several patients (cases 12 and 13) (6, 17, 21, 32, 58, 76, 118, 186).

Two reports describe the association of primary myxedema with galactorrhea in women with large pituitary tumors. One had amenorrhea (100), the other had menorrhagia (155). It was postulated that the tumors developed secondary to chronic overproduction of TSH with subsequent disruption of PIH effected by compression of the pituitary stalk. Brown *et al* (31) described a 13-year-old girl with hypothyroidism, galactorrhea and irregular menses. Roentgenograms of the skull showed the sella to be at the upper limits of normal in size and a pneumoencephalogram revealed a "suggestion" of a suprasellar mass. Regular menses occurred and lactation ceased with thyroid replacement.

An exciting alternative explanation for the association of galactorrhea with primary myxedema is suggested by studies which have shown that administration of thyrotropin-releasing hormone (TRH) to man causes a large increase in serum prolactin (27, 71, 110, 131, 196). Kaplan *et al* (116) found the highest prolactin levels attained after TRH to be in two adolescent girls. This is consistent with the stimulating effect of estrogens on secretion and pituitary storage of prolactin. There is no rise in hGH after the administration of TRH supporting the concept of hPr and hGH as distinct hormones. Sachson *et al* (192) found that hPr will rise in response to administration of TRH even in isolated TSH deficiency, thus demonstrating that the hPr response is not dependent on TSH. Prolactin and TSH responses were greater in normal women than in normal men and both responses were greatly enhanced in hypothyroid patients and virtually abolished in hyperthyroid patients. Although elevated levels of prolactin have not been found consistently in primary myxedema, it is still possible that TRH may be identical or structurally similar to PRH.

Costin *et al* (43) reported the results of studies in two eight-year-old girls with myxedema and precocious puberty. Colostrum was expressed from the breasts of one of the girls. Except for sellas of normal size, these patients were similar to those reported by Van Wyk and Grumbach. Levels of LH, FSH, TSH, prolactin and estrogen were greatly elevated. All symptoms remitted after treatment with thyroid extract. The authors speculated that TRH was increased because of decreased amounts of thyroxin. Elevated plasma LH and FSH may have been the result of crossreactivity with TSH or of nonspecific stimulation of gonadotropin release at the pituitary or hypothalamic level. Elevated plasma prolactin may have resulted from TRH stimulation of the pituitary or, less likely, from interference with normal tonic suppression of prolactin secretion.

Zondek and co-workers (245) described what they have called an *anterior pituitary hyperhormonotrophic syndrome* occurring in six parous women. All six had thyrotoxic symptoms and a tendency to hypoglycemia. Menometrorrhagia of long duration was associated with uterine enlargement. Nonpuerperal galactorrhea was present. The patients had secondary symptoms of physical exhaustion, anemia and sterility. No evidence of pituitary tumor could be found. The authors postulated a state of cellular hyperplasia although no pathologic studies were done. Later, Jackson (109) described a similar case of a 37-year-old multipara with normal menses and galactorrhea after delivery in whom symptoms of hyperthyroidism subsequently developed. Forbes *et al* (65) mentioned two patients with the Chiari-Frommel syndrome and associated thyrotoxicosis.

Refetoff *et al* (179) reported the case of a woman with the Chiari-Frommel syndrome associated with primary adrenocortical insufficiency. Base-line levels of LH, FSH, TSH and GH were normal, but prolactin and ACTH were elevated. Prolactin levels responded appropriately to TRH stimulation and levodopa suppression. Steroid replacement resulted in return of menses and cessation of galactorrhea.

Adrenal carcinoma (23, 135, 168), testicular chorioepithelioma (41), male hypogonadism (233, 239) and pelvic surgery including hysterectomy (67, 77, 107, 191, 204) and salpingectomy (18, 77, 134, 191) have been associated with galactorrhea. Most cases were reported before sensitive hormonal assays became available; therefore the endocrine relationships remain obscure.

Briggs and Powell (*Calif Med, 111*:92, 1969) reported a case of

Chiari-Frommel syndrome in a patient who subsequently was found to have the Zollinger-Ellison syndrome, intermittent hypercalcemia, and a positive family history for endocrine tumors. This is the only reported association of Chiari-Frommel syndrome with multiple endocrine adenomatosis. The possibility of a subclinical pituitary tumor in this patient remains.

Turkington (220) recently reported two cases of nonendocrine neoplasms—one a bronchogenic carcinoma and the other a hypernephroma—which produced prolactin. Although only the patient with the latter tumor had galactorrhea, we anticipate additional reports of ectopic production of prolactin as the assays for prolactin become more widely available. It is evident, however, that production of prolactin by a tumor will not necessarily be accompanied by galactorrhea.

CHAPTER 9

DISTURBANCES OF THE THORACIC WALL ASSOCIATED WITH GALACTORRHEA

THE TRANSPORT OF MILK from the alveoli through the ducts to the nipples is effected by contraction of myoepithelial cells; this is known as *milk ejection* or the *let-down reflex* and is initiated by suckling or other stimuli to the nipples. The reflex is carried by the anterior and lateral branches of the fourth, fifth and sixth thoracic nerves to pathways in the CNS and ultimately to the hypothalamus (45, 87, 180). The efferent limb of this reflex is the release of oxytocin stimulating the myoepithelial cells to contract. In addition, the secretion of prolactin during lactation is maintained by suckling-induced removal of hypothalamic inhibition (12, 107, 242). Grosvenor (88) showed that suckling as well as stress causes the release of prolactin by inhibiting the release and, perhaps, the concomitant synthesis of PIH by hypothalamic neural elements.

Stimulation of the nerves supplying the anterior thoracic wall has produced galactorrhea not associated with other signs or symptoms. Knott (123), Seifert (199) and Sharp (201) reviewed earlier cases of lactation in the male and nonpuerperal female produced by stimulation of the nipples. Wieschhoff (240) reviewed the techniques of primitives in Africa, India, Indonesia, North America, South America and Polynesia for inducing lactation in grandmothers and nulliparous women. In addition to pounded hornets' larvae, millet beans, plant sap and various herbal concoctions both ingested and applied locally, the mainstay of treatment appeared to be suckling or other stimulation to the breasts. It is possible that some of the ingested material may have contained alkaloids or other compounds similar to the drugs known to be associated with galactorrhea. (See Chapter 10.) More recently, Gilbert (78) described the case of a woman who lactated

45

for 15 years after delivery; menses were normal. She thought one should continue lactating after pregnancy and therefore stimulated production of milk by expressing it manually every day. Slome (207) added his observations of four women ranging in age from 45 to 48 years who stimulated production of milk by suckling their grandchildren. Three of the women were premenopausal; no data were given on the fourth. Others have reported their observations of suckling-induced lactation (15, 25, 67, 162, 173). McDonald and Lerner (151) and Verbov (231) reported cases of lactation induced by persistent scratching and rubbing of breasts afflicted with atopic dermatitis.

Salkin and Davis (193) reported ten cases of galactorrhea after thoracotomy and pneumonectomy. Lactation was greater on the operated side, although both breasts usually were affected. Two patients were nulliparous. Lactation lasted from three to 27 months. All patients were premenopausal and menses were unaffected. Mechanical injury and inflammation of nerves after the operation were postulated to have stimulated the suckling reflex producing continuous stimulation of the neurogenic component of the lactation mechanism resulting in increased production of prolactin. Grossman and co-workers (87), Berger *et al* (22) and Richardson (181) reported four similar cases. One patient described by Grossman *et al* had some lactation up to six years after thoracotomy. Hartley and Schatten (95) reported lactation as a postoperative complication of augmentation mammoplasty in two women taking oral contraceptives.

Grimm (85) reported a case of galactorrhea after trauma to the chest. Berger *et al* (22) reported that a 45-year-old woman lactated bilaterally as a result of stimulation by rubbing a pruritic scar after healing of a left submammary laceration. Lactation and engorgement were temporarily relieved by intercostal nerve block. Aufses (11) reported the only case of abnormal lactation subsequent to unilateral radical mastectomy.

White (236) was unsuccessful in attempts to produce lactation by use of an electrically operated breast pump in three non-puerperal multiparous women, suggesting that factors other than mechanical stimulation must be involved in producing galactorrhea.

CHAPTER 10

DRUG - RELATED GALACTORRHEA

WITH THE INCREASING use of oral contraceptives reports have appeared describing associated inappropriate lactation. This side-effect occurs without regard to parity or length of drug ingestion (202). The onset of lactation may be during drug therapy (69, 84, 95, 102, 165, 171, 203, 219), coincidental with monthly withdrawal (185) or on cessation of use of oral contraceptives (33, 69, 107, 145, 165, 195, 219). Menstrual dysfunction may or may not ensue on discontinuation of the medication. Further studies utilizing prolactin assays may help to determine whether oral contraceptives do or do not (69, 70, 206) increase the incidence of galactorrhea. (See Chapter 1.)

It is noteworthy that although estrogen in physiologic doses has been shown to increase secretion of prolactin (153, 211) we are aware of no well-documented case of estrogen-induced galactorrhea, possibly due to the inhibitory effect of high estrogen levels on the mammary gland (53).

Abnormal lactation is a relatively infrequent side-effect of psychotropic drug therapy, but its incidence increases in proportion to the quantity of drug administered. Many workers have observed galactorrhea in female patients treated with chlorpromazine (Thorazine), usually with doses ranging from 25 to 150 mg daily (case 4) (13, 40, 44, 66, 103, 117, 147, 159, 171, 184, 212, 215, 218, 242). The incidence varied from 33 of 650 patients in Khazan and co-workers' series (117) to 18 of 50 patients in Tenenblatt and Spagno's series (215). Patients ranged in age from 20 to 42 years in the combined series. In addition to chlorpromazine, Hooper *et al* (103) reported cases of lactation associated with the use of thioridazine (Mellaril), trifluoperazine (Stelazine), prochlorperazine (Compazine), fluphenazine (Prolixin), meprobamate (Equanil) and combinations of the fore-

47

going drugs. Thioridazine, 300 mg daily, was the medication most
frequently producing lactation. Other psychotropic drugs, including phenothiazines, tricyclic antidepressants, butyrophenones,
thiaxanthene derivitives, meprobamate, chlordiazepoxide (Libri-
um) and reserpine (Serpasil) have been associated with abnormal lactation (Table 2-II). Pettinger *et al* (172), Vaidya and associates (229) and Frantz and Kleinberg (68) have reported
cases of lactation induced by methyldopa (Aldomet).

With psychotropic drug-induced galactorrhea, the breasts may
be swollen and appear turgid (see Frontispiece). Secretion may
come from one breast only but usually both breasts are affected.
Discharge of fluid may be spontaneous and profuse or manual expression may yield only sparse secretion. As with galactorrhea
from other causes, the type of secretion may vary from colostrum
to normal milk. Lactation tends to begin two to four weeks after
initiation of therapy and usually ceases when the drug is with-
drawn. Most such patients with galactorrhea have been in the re-
productive age group. Reports on the effect of these drugs on
menses vary, some showing that cycles are unaffected while others
indicate menstrual disturbances (214, 242). Apostolakis *et al*
(242) observed a higher incidence of psychotropic drug-induced
galactorrhea in women who have never lactated previously. They
also reported the occurrence of galactorrhea in six of 60 males
treated with psychotropic drugs.

Reserpine depletes the brain of catecholamines and prevents
their re-uptake by nerve endings, phenothiazines interfere with
the action of catecholamines at receptor sites and methyldopa inhibits the transformation of dopa into dopamine. The common
effect of these drugs is to decrease production of PIH thus abol-
ishing the hypothalamic inhibition of prolactin secretion (13,
117, 152, 154, 211, 212, 242). Frantz and Kleinberg (68) found
high concentrations of circulating prolactin in four endocrino-
logically normal men and women receiving high doses of chlorpromazine or imipramine. Others have demonstrated elevated
concentrations of serum prolactin after administration of various
psychotropic drugs (121, 221, 224, 242). Turkington (226) found
elevated prolactin levels up to 20 days after oral administration
of psychotropic drugs was discontinued.

Spironolactone (Aldactone®) and digitalis, which are known to produce gynecomastia, have no effect on serum prolactin and have not been reported to cause galactorrhea. Patients having conditions associated with gynecomastia but not with galactorrhea generally have not had elevated prolactin levels (66, 222, 233, 242).

CHAPTER 11

DIAGNOSTIC EVALUATION AND MANAGEMENT OF GALACTORRHEA

THE EXISTENCE OF GALACTORRHEA is established by history, physical examination and analysis of secretions as needed. It is not unusual for a patient to have galactorrhea but not be aware of its existence until it is found on physical examination. The physician in turn may not find galactorrhea unless he attempts to demonstrate it. Gently squeezing the breast below the nipple (Fig. 11-1 A) will usually bring forth evidence of galactorrhea, if it is present. However, at times, this will not evoke secretions even though galactorrhea exists, and a more productive maneuver is to press, with cupped hands, medially and upward on the entire breast (Fig. 11-1 B). Occasionally, the patient may be more adept than the examining physician in inducing secretions.

The examiner should appreciate, when causing the breast to yield its secretions, that the first milliliter or so of fluid may be clear or straw colored (Fig. 11-2 A). With persistence the fluid will become milky or creamy (Fig. 11-2 B). It should also be appreciated that, on examination, one breast may immediately produce milky or creamy fluid while the other may produce clear or straw-colored fluid to be followed by the typical milky or creamy secretion of galactorrhea.

Often an indication of the etiology can be obtained from a history of disease of the central nervous system, drug intake, operative procedures or excessive stimulation of the breasts and nipples. If amenorrhea is associated with galactorrhea, ingestion of psychotropic drugs, local trauma and excessive stimulation are less likely to be etiologic factors, and other causes should be considered.

Positive responses to the following questions should help to exclude causes of breast secretions other than galactorrhea: (1) Is the patient nulliparous or more than 12 months past delivery and has nursing been stopped for several months? (2) Is secretion present in both breasts? (3) Does the secretion occur spontaneously and is it easily expressed and nonintermittent? (4) Is the secretion milky without evidence of blood or pus? In some situations it may be necessary to stain the secretion for fat to verify galactorrhea.

In selected cases in which no cause is evident, certain studies may be indicated. A pituitary or suprasellar tumor sometimes may be detected only after repeated roentgenograms of the skull over several years. Visual fields should be plotted if there is any question of a sellar or suprasellar lesion. Estrogen levels should be evaluated by vaginal cytology, response to administration and withdrawal of progestational agents or estimation of the plasma level or urinary excretion of estrogens. These studies, together with the determination of levels of urinary gonadotropin excretion or plasma values for gonadotropins such as FSH and LH, are carried out in order to evaluate both ovarian and pituitary function. Values for urinary 17-ketosteroids, 17-hydroxycorticosteroids and plasma cortisol should be determined and thyroid function should be studied to rule out disorders and associated abnormalities of the adrenal cortex and thyroid and to evaluate pituitary function. In view of the similarity in the early clinical features of the various galactorrheal syndromes there is a definite need for repeated follow-up examinations to exclude the presence of CNS tumors when an explanation for the galactorrhea is not evident.

Tests for the suppression and stimulation of prolactin are being developed; these should prove helpful in evaluating anterior pituitary function in general as well as conditions associated with galactorrhea. Recent studies have shown the nonsuppressibility of serum prolactin levels during an oral glucose tolerance test in patients with prolactin-producing pituitary tumors. It has been suggested that use of this test might be valuable in distinguishing such tumors from other conditions associated with elevated levels of prolactin since levels in more benign disorders should suppress in response to induced hyperglycemia (66). However, others have failed to demonstrate a consistent decrease in serum prolactin after glucose loading in normal controls (242). Increased prolactin levels have been noted after stimulation by hypoglycemia with a threshold of about 10 mg glucose/dl (164, 241). In view of this low threshold, an insulin stimulation test might be risky. Findings by Turkington (225) indicate that failure of serum prolactin levels to decrease after administration of levodopa might be more useful in distinguishing prolactin-producing pituitary tumors from other causes of galactorrhea.

Kleinberg *et al* (121) and Turkington (224) demonstrated that a single intramuscular injection of chlorpromazine into normal human beings will evoke considerable elevation of serum prolactin values within 30 to 120 minutes. Patients with hypopituitarism showed little or no response to this test, which has been proposed as a method of evaluating anterior pituitary function and prolactin reserve. Kleinberg *et al* (121) noted that pretreatment with levodopa greatly inhibited the rise of prolactin after the administration of chlorpromazine, and that, in four patients with chronically elevated plasma prolactin, a single oral dose of levodopa produced a rapid decrease in the prolactin values. Friesen *et al* (71) confirmed these findings and summarized the possible applications of TRH, chlorpromazine and levodopa in evaluation of hypothalamic-pituitary function as follows:

> A response to TRH indicates the presence of functional pituitary tissue. The lack of a response to chlorpromazine suggests an hypothalamic disorder if the TRH response is normal. A failure to respond to L-Dopa would indicate that the pituitary is functioning autonomously and is no longer under hypothalamic control. If there is a response to L-Dopa along with elevated levels of serum prolactin it suggests that the "set point" for prolactin secretion has been adjusted upwards.

Buckman *et al (J Clin Endocrinol Metab, 36*:911, 1973) reported the use of water loading in the evaluation of hyperprolactinemia. They noted that neither basal serum prolactin concentrations nor response to administration of L-dopa allowed separation of hyperprolactinemia associated with a pituitary tumor from functional disorders. On the basis of observations that endogenous secretion of prolactin and administration of prolactin promoted antidiuresis, the authors attempted to suppress serum prolactin levels by oral water loading. They noted that normal subjects and those with functional galactorrhea responded with suppression of serum prolactin to less than 50% of base line while no patient with pituitary tumor showed significant suppression after water loading.

Turkington (224) has used the chlorpromazine test to delineate a new syndrome of isolated deficiency of prolactin secretion in two patients with failure to lactate after delivery. These patients, however, were not tested with TRH which could have helped to delineate primary pituitary from hypothalamic dysfunction.

Specific treatment as it applies to individual conditions has been discussed. Since spontaneous remission has been reported in Chiari-Frommel syndrome as well as in other conditions associated with lactation, any positive results of treatment must be interpreted with the possibility in mind that such treatment was instituted at the time when remission would have occurred spontaneously. In situations where no definitive treatment is available and the desirability for control for symptoms outweighs the potential danger of long-term drug therapy, levodopa currently appears to be the drug of choice for suppression of galactorrhea, though ergot derivatives deserve further clinical evaluation (Tables 11-I, 11-II and 11-III). When it becomes available, PIH may be effective clinically in inhibiting lactation.

Supportive measures should not be overlooked. As with physiologic lactation, galactorrhea is usually reduced significantly by the use of a tight garment over the breasts and by avoidance of breast manipulation. If the patient's sense of well-being is disturbed by lack of menses, cyclic therapy should be undertaken with estrogens and progesterone.

It is essential to have some knowledge of the etiology, possible treatment and progression of galactorrhea if only to reassure the apprehensive patients in the more benign cases and to ensure proper treatment of those patients whose lactation is merely the surface expression of more deep-seated disorders.

TABLE 11-I.
EFFECT OF TREATMENT ON GALACTORRHEA*: 54 PATIENTS WITH CHIARI-FROMMEL OR DEL CASTILLO SYNDROME

Treatment	Chiari-Frommel (30 pt)				Del Castillo (24 pt)			
	C	D	I	U	C	D	I	U
Estrogen	1 (2)	1 (150)		12 (39,56,86,114,134, 138,190,217,232)	1 (114)			5 (7,67,138,232,230)
Progesterone	2 (96)	1 (217)		3 (39,56,114)	1 (96)			2 (7,217)
Estrogen and progesterone				7 (9,34,56,86,132,190)				1 (217)
Androgen				3 (86,114,134)				1 (232)
Estrogen and androgen				1 (case 3)				
Glucocorticoid				1 (138)				
Thyroid preparation		1 (144)		2 (175) (case 3)				
Gonadotropins			1	1 (132)				
Clomiphene	2 (114, 203)	3 (114,176, 203)			3 (203)	1 (138)	1 (case 1)	1 (7)
Levodopa				1 (145)	5 (71,225)			
Ergot and alkaloid		2 (53,140)			1 (53)			
Wedge resection	1 (100)				1 (129)			3 (129,160)
Radiation to pituitary	1 (56)			1 (90)				1 (case 2)

More than one treatment was attempted in most cases because of infrequent successes. Therapy was initiated most often for amenorrhea, tumor or some other primary condition rather than for galactorrhea *per se*.

*Galactorrhea: C = ceased; D = decreased; I = increased; U = unchanged.

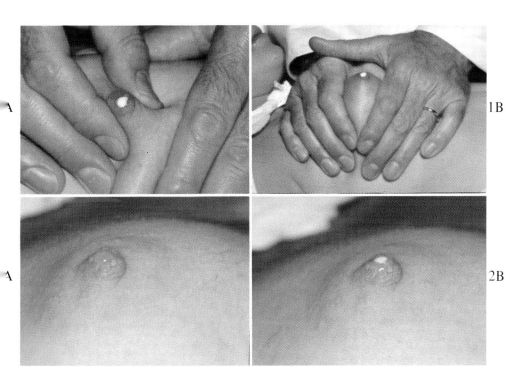

Figure 11-1. A) Squeezing the breast gently just below the nipple and then squeezing the nipple itself will usually demonstrate galactorrhea. B) Cupping both hands over the breast and pressing inward and upward may be necessary to demonstrate galactorrhea.

Figure 11-2. A) Note drop of straw-colored fluid on top of nipple. B) With further pressure, more creamy fluid, typical of galactorrhea, began to appear.

TABLE 11-II.
EFFECT OF TREATMENT ON GALACTORRHEA:* 72 PATIENTS WITH INTRACRANIAL TUMORS †‡§‖¶

Treatment	Chromophobe (12 pt)				Specified tumors (11 pt)				Miscellaneous and unspecified (50 pt)			
	C	D	I	U	C	D	I	U	C	D	I	U
Estrogen				1 (case 28)	1† (219)	2‡ (105) (232)		1‡ (67)		1 (65)		3 (case 30) (39,55)
Progesterone												2 (39,65)
Estrogen and progesterone										2 (81,142)		
Androgen									1 (91)			18 (150)
Glucocorticoid												2 (81)
Thyroid preparation									1 (14)			1 (case 28)
Gonadotropins		1 (71)										1 (81)
Levodopa									4 (225, 227)			5 (145, 225, 227)
Ergot and alkaloid										1 (140)		
Wedge resection												1 (236)

TABLE 11-II. (Continued)

Treatment	Chromophobe (12 pt)				Specified tumors (11 pt)				Miscellaneous and unspecified (50 pt)			
	C	D	I	U	C	D	I	U	C	D	I	U
Mastectomy												
Craniotomy	5 [161, 217, 244]	2 (case 12) [155]		1 [217]	2 [99, 170]			1‡ [46]	1§ [150]		1 (case 24)	4 (cases 28, 33) [108]
Radiation to pituitary				1 [244]		1‡ [46]		2‡ [67, 105]	16§§ (case 34) [21, 64, 108, 129]	4 (cases 30, 32, 38) [55]		8§ (cases 33, 36) [124, 130, 145, 150, 158, 244]
Craniotomy and radiation to pituitary		1 (case 26)	1 (case 27)		1∥ [183]	2∥ (case 20) [183]		1¶ (case 19)		1 (case 22)		1 (case 29)

More than one treatment was attempted in most cases because of infrequent successes. Therapy was initiated most often for amenorrhea, tumor or some other primary condition rather than for galactorrhea per se.

*Galactorrhea: C = ceased; D = decreased; I = increased; U = unchanged.

†Basophil (1 pt).

‡Acromegaly (4 pt).

§One male patient.

∥Nonacromegalic acidophilic adenoma (4 pt).

¶Craniopharyngioma (2 pt).

TABLE 11-III

EFFECT OF TREATMENT ON GALACTORRHEA:* 35 PATIENTS WITH MISCELLANEOUS CONDITIONS

Treatment	Sheehan's syndrome (2 pt)				Primary myxedema (14 pt)				Miscellaneous nontumor-associated conditions (19 pt)			
	C	D	I	U	C	D	I	U	C	D	I	U
Estrogen			1 [56]				1 [186]		3† [109, 233,245]			
Progesterone									1 [245]			
Estrogen and progesterone									1 [245]			
Androgen									6† [109, 233,245]			
Glucocorticoid and thyroid preparation	2 [56, 130]				1 [32]							
Thyroid preparation		1 [56]			11 (case 13) [17,31,43, 76,118,230]	2 [6,186]						
Growth hormone		1 [130]										
Gonadotropins									3 [245]			
Levodopa									7 [225]	1 [225]		
Ergot and alkaloid									4 [127]	1 [140]		
Mastectomy										1† [223]		

More than one treatment was attempted in most cases because of infrequent successes.

Therapy was initiated most often for amenorrhea, tumor or some other primary condition rather than for galactorrhea *per se.*

*Galactorrhea: C = ceased; D = decreased; I = increased; U = unchanged.

†One male patient.

CHAPTER 12

REPORT OF 41 CASES RECENTLY
ENCOUNTERED AT MAYO CLINIC

THE FOLLOWING 41 CASES represent our experience with patients with galactorrhea subsequent to the Mayo Clinic experience reported in 1965 by Thompson and Kempers (217). It should be noted that this series is heavily weighted in favor of patients with tumors in and around the pituitary gland, because tumors of this type are of major interest to one of us (R.V.R.). Undoubtedly, many other patients with galactorrhea developing secondary to taking birth control pills or tranquilizers were seen at this clinic during this period, but did not come to our attention. Hence, the incidence of the various causes of galactorrhea can in no way be gleaned from this small, biased series.

The cases are reported in a sequence that we consider to be the most instructive in reviewing the vagaries of the conditions associated with galactorrhea (Table 12-I).

TABLE 12-I
CONDITIONS ASSOCIATED WITH GALACTORRHEA IN 41 PATIENTS

	Number of patients	Case numbers
Del Castillo syndrome	2	1, 2
Chiari-Frommel syndrome	1	3
Drug-associated galactorrhea	7	4-10
Male with intrasellar tumor	1	11
Myxedema	3	12-14
Acromegaly	3	15-17
Craniopharyngioma	3	18-20
Pinealoma	1	21
Astrocytoma	1	22
Postoperative meningioma	1	23
Forbes-Albright syndrome	16	24-39
Transient (stress-associated) galactorrhea	1	40
Idiopathic (normal menses)	1	41

REPORT OF CASES

Del Castillo Syndrome

Cases 1 and 2 represent examples of Del Castillo syndrome, and case 3 is an example of Chiari-Frommel syndrome.

Case 1.— A 19-year-old woman (gravida [G]-0) presented in November, 1969, complaining of amenorrhea and breast secretions. Breast development began at seven years of age and appearance of pubic and axillary hair at nine years. Because of failure to undergo menarche and the appearance of breast secretions, cyclic hormone therapy was begun in 1962 when she was 12 years of age and was continued to November, 1969, with resultant withdrawal bleeding. Secretions stopped once during therapy, but resumed.

Results of physical examination, except for expression of breast secretions, were normal. Work-up was essentially negative. Roentgenograms of the skull were normal. A course of clomiphene was given with resultant menses, but breast secretions increased and the medication was discontinued. The patient continued to have galactorrhea but no menses up to the time of her last visit in August, 1971.

Comment.—Follow-up of this patient's condition has not been long enough to rule out an intrasellar or suprasellar tumor, especially since she never experienced menarche.

Case 2. — A 23-year-old nulliparous woman, seen in August, 1958, complained of recurrent sore throat for 14 years. Menarche was at 12 years of age with regular menses thereafter until January, 1956 (age, 21 years) when menses ceased. Injection of hormones produced withdrawal bleeding several times, but eventually they were without effect. On questioning, she stated that since the onset of amenorrhea, whitish secretions occasionally had exuded from the nipples.

Examination revealed bilateral breast secretions (see Frontispiece *A*), an atrophic uterus, small firm ovaries and an anestrogenic vaginal smear. Tests of 24-hour collection of urine for estrogen and gonadotropins gave negative results. Roentgenograms of the head did not show evidence of abnormality. Cyclic administration of estrogen and progesterone failed to produce withdrawal bleeding.

The patient was seen elsewhere in 1960 and a diagnosis of sellar enlargement was made. Cobalt-60 therapy was given to the region of the sella. When she was seen again at this clinic in 1967, she reported that spontaneous menses had occurred every other month in 1965 and every month since 1966. Breast secretions continued. Tomography of the sella turcica and examination of the visual fields did not reveal an abnormality. Review of roentgenograms made elsewhere in 1960 did not confirm, in our opinion, a sellar abnormality.

Comment.—This is one of the rare cases of galactorrhea and amenorrhea without evidence of pituitary tumor treated with radiation to the sella. The relationship of return of menses to radiation therapy can only be speculative.

Dowling *et al* (56) reported the case of a patient who had irregular menses and lactation for four years after delivery. A dose of 4,000 R was delivered to the sella, although roentgenograms of the head and studies of visual fields were without abnormality. Lactation ceased after radiation therapy. Haskins *et al* (96) reported the case of a patient with presumed Chiari-Frommel syndrome who failed to respond to pituitary radiation. Ashkar (9) showed no immediate effect on lactation through "stimulation" of the pituitary gland with 252 R in a patient with Chiari-Frommel syndrome.

Chiari-Frommel Syndrome

Case 3. — A 38-year-old housewife (G-V, Para [P]-5) presented in December, 1964, with persistent lactation and amenorrhea since her last delivery six years previously. She had had five normal deliveries, but had not nursed any of her infants. After the birth of her last child, her breasts failed to return to their prepartum size and menses did not resume. For three years her breasts produced enough secretions to require the use of nursing pads, but in the subsequent three years the amount had diminished considerably. Libido was reduced and she had gained 11 kg. There was a history of several hospitalizations for psychiatric complaints. Various medications including testosterone enanthate and estradiol valerate (Deladumone®) and a thyroid preparation had been prescribed, none of which had altered her breast secretions. A diagnosis of schizophrenia had been made.

Physical examination revealed an obese woman with decreased affect. Both breasts were full and milky fluid was easily expressed. The uterus was sounded to a depth of 6 cm, but on endometrial biopsy no tissue was obtained. Roentgenograms of the head showed a normal sella. The visual fields were normal.

Comment.—This is a typical example of Chiari-Frommel syndrome. Such patients may have psychiatric problems. The patient's breasts remained turgid for a number of years. While turgidity may be encountered with any of the conditions associated with galactorrhea, it is our impression that turgidity of the breasts is seen more frequently in drug-associated galactorrhea.

Drug-Associated Galactorrhea

Cases 4 through 9 present examples of galactorrhea associated with the ingestion of drugs.

Case 4. — A 35-year-old housewife (G-IV, P-2, abortions [Ab]-2) presented in April, 1963, with a complaint of discharge from the breasts during the preceding year. Menarche had occurred at 11 years of age with subsequent normal menses. Her last pregnancy was in 1959. The patient had a long history of neuroses. In 1962, after she had taken tranylcypromine (Parnate®) and chlorpromazine in large doses for two months, profuse milky secretions issued from the breasts but her menses continued. The use of chlorpromazine was discontinued with some decrease in the secretions. Subsequently, she took tranylcypromine and chlorpromazine intermittently. Secretions persisted with increased production accompanied by engorgement of the breasts at the time of ovulation and just prior to menses. Except for a small amount of milky secretion expressed from each breast, physical examination and laboratory findings were normal.

Comment.—The onset of galactorrhea was associated with the use of tranquilizers, which is a well-recognized cause of abnormal lactation.

Case 5. — A 35-year-old unmarried woman presented at the Mayo Clinic in January, 1963, with increasing nervousness, anxiety and depression of four years' duration. In addition, she complained of secretions from both breasts, vaginal discharge and gain in weight.

For the preceding two years the patient had been treated for mental symptoms with electroshock therapy and thioridazine. Somewhat more than a year before her admission to this clinic both breasts had enlarged slightly and had constantly produced a yellowish secretion. The menses remained regular. She had recently gained 14 kg. For three weeks prior to her admission, she had taken 25 mg of chlorotrianisene (Tace®) three times daily for her breast secretions without effect.

Physical findings included hirsutism and seborrhea with a spontaneous secretion of milky fluid from each breast. An elevation in protein-bound iodine and depressed uptake of triiodothyromine by erythrocytes were presumed due to the cholorotrianisene. Results of other laboratory tests were normal.

Comment.—Thioridazine has previously been associated with galactorrhea (103, 203). In this case, the inconvenience of galactorrhea was minor compared to the beneficial effect of the drug and, therefore, the use of thioridazine was continued.

Case 6. — A 36-year-old housewife (G-II, P-1, Ab-1) presented in November, 1966, complaining of bilateral hip pain. Menarche had occurred at 12 years of age with subsequent normal menses. In 1963, after a spontaneous abortion at three months, she noted the onset of lactation which persisted. She was taking meprobamate at the time and continued to take this drug until 1966 when the prescription was changed to thioridazine. Menses remained essentially normal.

Except for evidence of emotional instability and presence of breast secretions, results of physical examination were normal. No sellar abnormality could be found.

Comment.—Galactorrhea associated with treatment with meprobamate has been reported previously (103). In this patient it persisted when meprobamate was discontinued and thioridazine was given.

Case 7. — A 23-year-old housewife (G-II, P-2) was admitted to the Mayo Clinic in October, 1971, complaining of amenorrhea and galactorrhea since the birth of her last child in July, 1970. Menarche began at 12 years of age. She nursed her first child for two months, but stopped when she was given aprobarbital (Alurate®). Menses returned and lactation ceased. After her second pregnancy she nursed the infant for two weeks, but stopped when she started to take 300 mg of thioridazine daily. Over the ensuing months 75 mg of nortriptyline (Aventyl®) daily and 15 mg of trifluoperazine (Stelazine) daily were added. Menses failed to return and spontaneous copious lactation persisted. She remained under psychiatric care, which had been started several years previously for her obsessive-compulsive symptoms.

Physical examination was notable in that copious amounts of milk were easily expressed from her breasts. Roentgenograms, including tomograms, failed to show sellar abnormality.

Comment.—The use of tranquilizing drugs appears to have sustained lactation in this patient, whose case would otherwise be a typical example of Chiari-Frommel syndrome.

Case 8. — A 22-year-old housewife (G-0) presented in February, 1967, complaining of amenorrhea for the preceding 18 months. Secondary sex characteristics appeared at age 12 and menarche soon thereafter. Menses occurred every 35 to 39 days with two days of scanty flow. There was no dysmenorrhea or intermenstrual spotting. In May, 1965, she was given oral contraceptives and intramuscular estrogens for regulation of menses. Menses became regular but amount of flow did not change. On discontinuing the use of oral contraceptives in December, 1965, she had no spontaneous menses and bilateral milky breast secretions developed accompanied by pain and tenderness. The amount of milk varied with occasional spontaneous flow. She also experienced frequent occipital headaches.

Physical examination revealed well-developed, moderately cystic breasts from which thick white secretions could be expressed in small amounts. The uterus was small though it sounded to normal depth. Endometrial biopsy revealed atrophic endometrium. Roentgenograms of the skull were normal. The results of laboratory studies, including serum protein-bound iodine and values for urinary ketosteroids, ketogenic steroids and estrogens were normal; urinary pituitary gonadotropins, however, were undetectable.

Because she was eager to conceive, therapy with clomiphene (100 mg daily for five days) was started on April 15, 1967. On day 14 she had a biphasic temperature curve. Galactorrhea stopped completely a few days later. A pregnancy test was positive on June 13, 1967. She delivered twins on December 19, 1967. Postpartum she failed to menstruate and profuse lactation persisted.

Comment.—Amenorrhea and galactorrhea initially associated with use of oral contraceptives persisted after an intervening pregnancy. Such recurrences are more typical of the Chiari-Frommel syndrome and suggest primary hypothalamic dysfunction.

Case 9. — A 29-year-old housewife (G-I, P-2) came to the Mayo Clinic in January, 1972, complaining of severe headaches, weakness, lightheadedness and intermittent visual changes. In 1969 a diagnosis of Cushing's syndrome secondary to bilateral adrenocortical hyperplasia had been made elsewhere on the basis of typical physical findings and confirmatory laboratory tests. She was treated with 4,000 R of radiation therapy to the sella with gradual remission of symptoms. Menses failed to occur after treatment but she became pregnant after a course of clomiphene and delivered twins in April, 1971. She did not nurse her infants. Postpartum she took oral contraceptives which resulted in withdrawal bleeding but she had no menses after discontinuing the use of contraceptives in August, 1971. The symptoms with which she finally presented to this clinic developed over the ensuing months.

Physical examination revealed generalized obesity. Several drops of milk were easily expressed from both breasts. The patient had been unaware of breast secretion. Psychologic testing showed evidence of depression. Steroid determinations were in the low normal range without diurnal variation. Other tests including roentgenograms of the skull, echoencephalogram, electroencephalogram and visual fields were normal.

Comment.—The association of Cushing's syndrome due to adrenocortical hyperplasia with galactorrhea has been reported (129, 203, 244). Since both of these conditions may be associated with hypothalamic dysfunction, their occurrence in the same patient is not unexpected.

Galactorrhea in Males

In case 10, galactorrhea in a male was associated with the administration of an androgenic compound.

Case 10. — A 30-year-old man was known since November, 1966, to have carcinoma that had metastasized to the lungs and brain. The primary site was not determined. In March, 1967, he complained of tender breasts with secretions for approximately one month. He had been taking 10 mg of fluoxymesterone (Halotestin®) three times daily since November, 1966.

Whitish secretions could be expressed from each breast. Funduscopic examination revealed bilateral choked disks. Roentgenograms of the skull showed evidence of erosion of the floor and dorsum of the sella presumably secondary to increased intracranial pressure.

Comment.—Galactorrhea in men is distinctly unusual. Serosanguineous secretions associated with testosterone therapy have been noted (48). The whitish secretions of this patient make it likely that true galactorrhea was present. In addition to receiving androgens, the patient had metastases to the region of the sella and to the lungs. It is not known if the tumor was producing prolactin or if metastasis to the hypothalamus may have inhibited the release of PIH. Hence, one or more factors may have played a role in the genesis of the galactorrhea.

Case 11. — A 47-year-old man presented at the Mayo Clinic in March, 1972, for evaluation of chronic recurrent headaches. He had been first seen at this clinic in January, 1957, for evaluation of a nodule in the left breast that was subsequently removed surgically and reported as *adenofibromatous hyperplasia of the male breast featuring more than the usual amount of epithelial hyperplasia.* There had been no history of discharge from the breast.

In January, 1962, he presented with a subareolar mass in the right breast, which had first been noted six weeks previously He reported that two weeks previously a brownish discharge had come from the nipple on manipulation. This mass was removed subsequently at his local hospital.

In October, 1968, a roentgenogram of the skull taken for evaluation of recurrent headaches showed a calcified sellar mass. Subsequent testing including carotid angiograms did not reveal evidence of extrasellar extension. There was evidence of mild hypopituitarism. No specific antitumor therapy was used but he was given 2.5 mg of prednisone twice daily, 0.2 mg of sodium levothyroxine (Synthroid®) daily and a 200-mg intramuscular injection of testosterone enanthate (Delatestryl®) every three weeks as replacement therapy.

Evaluation in March, 1972, did not reveal evidence of tumor growth or other organic cause for his recurrent headaches. He had taken chlorpromazine (Thorazine) for an unknown period several years previously, but his recent medications had been limited to endocrine replacement therapy plus ergotamine tartrate and caffeine (Cafergot®), diazepam (Valium®), and meperidine (Demerol®) on an irregular basis for treatment of headache. He had discontinued the use of testosterone because of breast enlargement. During his physical examination, however, a small button of breast tissue was palpated under each nipple and multiple drops of milk were expressed from the right breast.

Comment.—Several factors may have contributed to the appearance of galactorrhea in this man, including therapy with chlorpromazine and testosterone and the presence of a pituitary tumor. In addition, the history of gynecomastia indicated a basic underlying condition that could have made his breasts more conducive to milk production.

GALACTORRHEA IN PATIENTS WITH MYXEDEMA.—Case 12 is one of galactorrhea associated with primary myxedema.

Case 12. — A 23-year-old housewife (G-I, P-1) seen in June, 1969, complained of galactorrhea and amenorrhea. Menarche occurred at 13 years of age with regular menses until her pregnancy in 1966. Delivery was normal. Administration of oral contraceptives was started immediately after delivery and continued until October, 1968. Although she did not nurse her infant, milk production persisted, necessitating the use of breast pads. Lactation increased somewhat for a time after the use of oral contraceptives was discontinued, but subsequently diminished. Spontaneous menses did not resume after use of the drug was discontinued.

Physical examination revealed generalized melanosis. Milky fluid was expressed from each nipple. Roentgenograms of the skull were negative. Examination of the visual fields was normal. Laboratory results were consistent with a diagnosis of primary myxedema (total serum thyroxine, 1.3 μg/dl; free serum thyroxine, 0.2 ng/dl; uptake of triiodothyronine, 8.5%; and TSH >82 μU/ml). Thyroid replacement was instituted. On follow-up in March, 1972, regular menses had resumed although lactation continued.

Comment.—The association of primary myxedema with amenorrhea-galactorrhea has been well documented (6, 21, 32, 76, 118, 186). Pregnancy and the use of oral contraceptives cloud the picture in this case.

Case 13. — A 17-year-old girl was admitted to the Mayo Clinic in November, 1966, for evaluation of retarded growth since the age of 12. She had been the tallest girl in her class until that time, but since age 13 she had grown only 2 cm. Menarche occurred at 13 years of age and menses had been regular since age 16. She had mild intolerance to cold.

Examination revealed a normally proportioned girl 150 cm tall. Facial features appeared younger than 17 years. She had early adolescent breasts with much nipple development and minimal acinar growth. There was slight pigmentation of the nipples and areolae. Axillary hair was normal but pubic hair was scant. The uterus was half normal size; no adnexal masses were palpable and the labia minora were hyptertrophied.

On subsequent examination six months later her hair had become dry and hard to manage, her skin was cold and sallow, her face appeared puffy and her reflexes were slow. On further questioning she admitted that since she was 15 years of age she had had discharge from both breasts which stained her clothes on occasion.

Laboratory examination revealed low protein-bound iodine and elevated values for thyroid stimulating hormones consistent with a diagnosis of primary myxedema. Roentgenograms of the head showed no evidence of abnormality.

Thyroid replacement therapy resulted in alleviation of the patient's symptoms, including cessation of the breast discharge and slight additional growth.

Comment.—This patient had galactorrhea associated with juvenile myxedema. As in most reported cases (Table 11-III), thyroid replacement alleviated the breast secretions.

Case 14. — A 12-year-old girl was seen in April, 1965, for evaluation of slow growth and development since early infancy. Several physicians had been consulted over the years and at five years of age she had been placed on one-half grain of desiccated thyroid daily, which resulted in more rapid growth for some time. Besides short

stature her symptoms included dry, hard-to-manage hair, easy fatig-
ability and mental dullness.

Examination revealed a small, mentally dull girl 142 cm tall. She
had a deep voice, dry hair, slow reflexes, stubby hands and feet and
a short trunk. Breasts contained only a small amount of acinar tissue. A few hairs were present on each labium.

Laboratory examination revealed low values for protein-bound
iodine. Roentgenograms of the skull revealed evidence of an enlarged
sella. Bone age was consistent with her chronologic age.

Thyroid replacement therapy was initiated and resulted in complete resolution of her symptoms and further growth. Menarche occurred at 15 years of age.

At a later interview she volunteered that she had had a milky
breast discharge prior to initiation of thyroid replacement; there had
been no spontaneous discharge since taking thyroid hormone, but she
occasionally noted some yellow secretions on manipulation. No change
in sella configuration was noted on roentgenograms of the skull at the
time of her last examination in September, 1972.

Comment.—This patient had myxedema, galactorrhea and an
enlarged sella, characteristics suggestive of the overlap syndrome,
which was first described by Van Wyk and Grumbach (230). (See
Chapter 8.)

Galactorrhea and Acromegaly

Cases 15, 16 and 17 are examples of galactorrhea in patients
with acromegaly. This association has also been found in males
with acromegaly (188, 210).

Case 15. — A 42-year-old housewife (G-VI, P-4, Ab-2) presented at
the Mayo Clinic in September, 1971, complaining of lightheadedness.
After several years of slowly evolving acromegalic features, a diagnosis
of acromegaly had been made elsewhere. A course of cobalt radiation
was given in October, 1970. Because of persistent high plasma values
for growth hormone, craniotomy was performed in January, 1971,
resulting in the excision of an eosinophilic adenoma.

Menses had been irregular since 1968. On close questioning she
revealed a history of persistent lactation, at least since the birth of
her last child 12 years previously, and possibly since the birth of her
first child 22 years previously. Biopsy of the right breast had been
performed six years previously because of continuing secretions, but
no specific diagnosis was given.

Examination revealed typical acromegalic features. Several drops
of milky fluid were expressed from the left nipple. The right breast,

which was deformed from the previous biopsy, produced no secretions. Laboratory results and roentgenographic evidence of an enlarged sella were consistent with acromegaly. Mammograms appeared normal.

Comment.—From the history it was not clear whether galactorrhea and acromegaly began about the same time, or whether galactorrhea preceded the onset of acromegaly.

Case 16. — A 35-year-old housewife (G-III, P-3) presented at this clinic in January, 1971, for evaluation of a suspected intracranial tumor. Her last delivery had been seven years previously. Menses were normal until September, 1968, when amenorrhea occurred. Thereafter she experienced progressive weakness, fatigue, gain in weight, deepening voice, enlargement of her nose, hands and feet, numbness and tingling of her fingers, increased perspiration, hirsutism, loss of libido and mild discomfort in the left side of her head.

Physical examination revealed classic features of acromegaly. In addition, milk was expressed from each breast. Laboratory evaluation revealed sellar enlargement and a slight right superior temporal defect on visual field examination. A pituitary adenoma was removed at craniotomy. She received a course of cobalt radiation in the postoperative period. Galactorrhea ceased but menses did not return.

Case 17. — A 35-year-old housewife (G-IV, P-3, Ab-1) was admitted to the Mayo Clinic in April, 1962, complaining of amenorrhea subsequent to delivery of her last child in December, 1960. Parturition was normal without excess hemorrhage or shock. She did not nurse her infant. The ensuing amenorrhea was complete except for three episodes of withdrawal bleeding induced by hormones. There had been no hot flushes. Libido had decreased. Since her delivery, milky fluid could be expressed from each breast. Further questioning revealed that her ring size and shoe size had steadily increased over the preceding several years.

Physical examination revealed coarse facial features. Her hands and fingers were broader than normal. Milky fluid was readily expressed from both breasts. Vaginal smear showed a resting epithelium. Pelvic examination revealed a normal-sized uterus, but biopsy showed an atrophic endometrium. Photographs showed acromegalic changes over the previous five years.

Roentgenograms of the head revealed slight enlargement of the sella. Fundi and visual fields were normal. She was given a course of cobalt radiation.

Comment.—Postpartum amenorrhea and galactorrhea associated with acromegaly have been reported previously (14, 46, 49, 105, 232),

Galactorrhea and Craniopharyngioma

Cases 18, 19 and 20 represent examples of galactorrhea associated with craniopharyngioma.

Case 18. — A 33-year-old housewife (G-V, P-5) admitted to the Mayo Clinic in July, 1966, complained of severe headaches and amenorrhea since November, 1961. Menarche was at 14 years of age with regular menses thereafter. Her fifth child was born in November, 1961. Menses failed to return after her delivery. She had had persistent lactation since delivery and had had some withdrawal bleeding with cyclic hormone therapy. Bitemporal hemianopsia was found by her ophthalmologist in July, 1966, and it was then that she was referred to this clinic.

Roentgenograms of the head did not show evidence of abnormality, but fundus and visual field examinations showed optic atrophy and bitemporal hemianopsia. Angiograms showed evidence of an intrasellar tumor with suprasellar extension. Surgery resulted in subtotal resection of a cystic craniopharyngioma.

Case 19. — A 42-year-old housewife (G-IV, P-4) was seen at the Mayo Clinic in February, 1969. Menarche was at 12 years of age and was followed by normal menses until November, 1967, when she had spontaneous onset of amenorrhea, engorgement of breasts, galactorrhea and loss of libido not related to pregnancy. In May, 1968, she noted deterioration of her vision and onset of recurrent headaches. In October, 1968, polyuria and polydipsia developed.

Examination revealed decreased axillary but normal pubic hair. Breasts were full and milk was expressed from both. Roentgenograms of the skull appeared normal but examination of the visual fields revealed a right homonymous hemianopsia. Fractional pneumoencephalography showed a suprasellar mass (3 by 2 cm). Percutaneous aspiration confirmed a supratentorial, cystic craniopharyngioma. A course of cobalt-60 radiation was given. Galactorrhea persisted at the time of her last examination in June, 1969.

Case 20. — A 21-year-old housewife (G-I, P-1) was admitted to the Mayo Clinic in July, 1962, complaining of persistent lactation, amenorrhea, excessive gain in weight, visual loss and headaches. Menarche had occurred at 12 years of age with regular menses until her pregnancy in 1959. After the normal delivery of a full-term infant in May, 1960, she nursed the infant for three weeks. A milky discharge persisted and menses did not recur. From the beginning of her pregnancy until six months after delivery she had gained a total of 32 kg. Since the winter of 1960, she had noted daily headaches and deterioration of vision.

Examination revealed great obesity. The breasts were full of a milky secretion that could be expressed easily from both nipples. Visual field testing showed a bilateral inferior field loss due to involvement of the optic disk. Roentgenograms of the head revealed a calcified tumor above the sella. A right transfrontal craniotomy resulted in the removal of a supratentorial, cystic craniopharyngioma. Radiation therapy was administered postoperatively.

Galactorrhea, amenorrhea and obesity persisted after the operation. Visual fields improved and headaches did not recur. When the patient was last seen in January, 1972, it was still possible to express a drop of milky fluid from each nipple, but she did not have the spontaneous flow of fluid that she had had previously.

Comment.—Galactorrhea began in the postpartum period in cases 18 and 20. This condition has been noted in at least three of five previously reported cases in which the patients had craniopharyngioma and galactorrhea (5, 21, 38, 90, 108). This sequence could readily lead to a mistaken diagnosis of Chiari-Frommel syndrome unless the presence of the craniopharyngioma was recognized.

Galactorrhea and Other Suprasellar Tumors

Cases 21, 22 and 23 are examples of galactorrhea occurring in association with pinealoma, astrocytoma or surgical removal of a parasellar meningioma respectively.

Case 21. — A 36-year-old housewife (G-IV, P-4) was seen at the Mayo Clinic in August, 1966, because of headaches and visual difficulty. Menses had been normal prior to her last pregnancy in 1963. After her delivery, lactation continued although she did not nurse the infant. After two months of amenorrhea, she started taking oral contraceptives; withdrawal bleeding occurred after each cycle. She stopped taking oral contraceptives in August, 1965, and no spontaneous menstrual periods occurred subsequently. Small amounts of breast secretion continued. For the preceding two years, she had noted increasing polyuria and polydipsia. Loss of libido and decreased growth of sexual hair had developed over the preceding several months. In June, 1966, she had the sudden onset of bitemporal hemianopsia.

Examination revealed diminished axillary and pubic hair as well as an atrophic vagina and uterus. Bitemporal hemianopsia was confirmed on visual field examination. Roentgenograms of the skull revealed evidence of erosion of the sella. Fractional pneumoencephalograms showed a midline suprasellar mass. Subtotal resection of a malignant pinealoma (seminoma type), both intrasellar and suprasellar, was accomplished and followed by a course of cobalt-60 therapy. Amenorrhea and galactorrhea continued.

Comment.—Persistence of galactorrhea for extended periods after discontinuing a drug that may be associated with amenorrhea and galactorrhea should arouse suspicion of an underlying process.

Case 22. — A 28-year-old housewife (G-0) presented in April, 1966, for radiation therapy after removal of an intracranial tumor. Menarche occurred at 12 years of age with irregular menses until 1962. Oral contraceptives were taken from December, 1962, to February, 1965, when they were discontinued because of profuse, spontaneous lactation of two months' duration. Subsequently she had no spontaneous menses. Evaluation elsewhere revealed evidence of intracranial tumor. Craniotomy revealed an astrocytoma of the third ventricle and right optic tract.

Examination was unremarkable except for galactorrhea. Roentgenograms of the skull showed evidence of erosion beneath the right anterior clinoid. Visual field testing revealed incongruous left homonymous hemianopsia. Postoperative radiation therapy was given. Slight galactorrhea persisted until the last examination in October, 1969. Withdrawal bleeding was produced with cyclic use of a conjugated estrogen (Premarin®).

Comment.—As far as we are aware this is the only reported case of amenorrhea and galactorrhea associated with an astrocytoma.

Case 23. — A 27-year-old housewife (G-II, P-2) presented in December, 1962, complaining of impaired vision in her left eye. Sudden onset of blurred vision was noted in the eighth month of her second pregnancy. The change was not progressive and she had had a normal term delivery in October, 1962. Spontaneous menses resumed and lactation ceased. She had had severe, recurrent headaches for the preceding ten years.

Visual field testing revealed a superior temporal quadrantic defect on the left. No evidence of abnormality appeared on roentgenograms of the head. In January, 1963, a meningioma involving the left anterior clinoid was removed. The tumor was both intrasellar and suprasellar and impinged on both optic nerves.

Surgical treatment was followed by evidence of panhypopituitarism and diabetes insipidus and by the onset of lactation. She had had a spontaneous menstrual period immediately after the operation, but no recurrence thereafter. When last seen in October, 1964, she was having withdrawal bleeding on cyclic therapy with stilbestrol. Her breasts were full and spontaneously discharged milky fluid.

Comment.—To our knowledge, no case of galactorrhea subsequent to surgical resection of a meningioma has been reported, although this condition has been encountered after section of the pituitary stalk (51, 59).

Galactorrhea Associated With Chromophobe Adenoma

Cases 24 through 29 are those of patients who had galactorrhea and surgical treatment for chromophobe adenoma of the pituitary. Cases 30 through 39 are those of patients who had galactorrhea and evidences of an intrasellar tumor but who did not have an operation. The diagnosis in each of these 16 cases falls within the current definition of Forbes-Albright syndrome.

In reviewing these cases note especially that there was frequently a long interval between the onset of symptoms and the diagnosis of intrasellar tumor and also that commonly the patients' histories initially suggested the presence of Chiari-Frommel syndrome or Del Castillo syndrome and then terminated with the discovery of an intrasellar tumor.

Case 24. — A 31-year-old unmarried woman (G-0) presented in December, 1958, with complaints of galactorrhea, amenorrhea and obesity. For eight years she had had a white discharge from the right breast and for the past two years, considerable secretion from the left breast but only slight amounts from the right. Seven years previously her menstrual periods became irregular, then ceased completely. She had gained 23 kg in the preceding four years. Treatment with desiccated thyroid for two years was without effect.

Physical examination revealed an obese woman with somewhat cystic breasts. A white secretion was expressed from both. Laboratory evaluation revealed 24-hour urinary gonadotropins of 0 rat units (RU). The sella was enlarged and examination of the visual fields showed a lower nasal quadrant defect on the left. Right transfrontal craniotomy revealed an intrasellar and supratentorial chromophobe adenoma. Breast secretions increased in the immediate postoperative period then decreased subsequently; they were present at the time of her last examination in 1968.

Comment.—This case can be considered a classic example of Forbes-Albright syndrome.

Case 25. — A 35-year-old housewife (G-III, P-2, Ab-1) presented at this clinic in November, 1962, complaining of headaches and increasing visual loss for the preceding two months.

After her first full-term pregnancy in 1956, she nursed her infant for eight weeks. On weaning the child, her menses returned, but lactation persisted although secretions were evident only on manual expression. In 1959, after her second full-term pregnancy, she did not nurse her infant but continued to lactate and remained amenorrheic.

On examination, small amounts of milky fluid could be expressed from both breasts. Testing of visual fields revealed bitemporal hemianopsia. Evidence of an enlarged sella was demonstrated on roentgenograms of the skull. Right transfrontal craniotomy was performed with removal of a chromophobe adenoma.

On follow-up examination through August, 1964, only a drop of milky fluid could be expressed from each nipple. The patient was having withdrawal bleeding on cyclic therapy with stilbestrol.

Comment.—While the history was initially consistent with the symptoms of Chiari-Frommel syndrome, the patient eventually was found to have an intrasellar tumor (Forbes-Albright syndrome).

Case 26. — A 39-year-old housewife (G-VI, P-6) presented on October 26, 1965, because that day she experienced sudden onset of severe pain in the head and neck. Her last child was born in 1959. She did not nurse it but continued to have milky secretions. Menses ceased one year after delivery and she had had only one spontaneous menstrual period since.

Evaluation of the patient revealed bloody cerebrospinal fluid. A carotid angiogram indicated a suprasellar mass. Right frontal craniotomy was performed with removal of a pituitary chromophobe adenoma extending into the right frontal lobe and the right middle fossa. There was hemorrhage into the right frontal lobe. Cobalt-60 radiation was given. Galactorrhea continued, but at a diminished rate.

Comment.—It cannot be overemphasized that galactorrhea and amenorrhea without apparent cause should arouse suspicion of the presence of an intrasellar or suprasellar tumor.

Case 27. — A 22-year-old housewife (G-II, P-2) presented in May, 1969, complaining of headaches. Her history was unremarkable until November, 1963, with the birth of her second child. She was given medication to stop lactation but milk production persisted and menses did not return.

Examination revealed obesity. A milky secretion could be readily expressed from large breasts. Roentgenograms of the head revealed evidence of sellar enlargement with suprasellar extension. Examination of the visual fields showed bitemporal hemianopsia. Right frontal craniotomy was performed with subtotal removal of a chromophobe adenoma followed subsequently by radiation therapy. On follow-up in August, 1971, the breasts were still full of milk that could be expressed easily.

Comment.—This is another example of Forbes-Albright syndrome beginning as seemingly typical Chiari-Frommel syndrome.

Case 28. — A 22-year-old nulliparous woman presented in July, 1951, complaining of amenorrhea. Menarche occurred at 11 years of age with normal menses until they ceased spontaneously in 1949. Spontaneous lactation also occurred in 1949 and she gained 40 kg. She was given desiccated thyroid without effect.

Examination at this clinic in 1951 revealed obesity and a male escutcheon. Laboratory evaluation gave normal results. Roentgenograms of the skull were without evidence of abnormality. Estrogen (Premarin) was prescribed and produced withdrawal bleeding. After eight months, normal menses resumed.

The patient returned in April, 1954, complaining of headaches and visual loss. Menses had ceased five months previously and she did not have withdrawal bleeding from estrogen. Physical examination revealed obesity, oily skin, galactorrhea and bitemporal hemianopsia. Bilateral carotid angiograms showed a tumor above the tuberculum sella. The 24-hour urinary gonadotropins were 0 RU. At operation a pituitary adenoma was found. Some breast secretions were still present when the patient was last seen at this clinic in February, 1970.

Comment.—This patient had typical Del Castillo syndrome for five years until symptoms of a pituitary tumor appeared.

Case 29. — A 21-year-old student (G-0) was referred to the Mayo Clinic in February, 1972, for treatment of a pituitary tumor.

Between the ages of eight and twelve years she had received adrenal steroids for treatment of nephrosis. Breasts and pubic hair developed by age 14 but she failed to menstruate. Desiccated thyroid and oral contraceptives were prescribed to induce menses. She experienced withdrawal bleeding only. The thyroid medication was fin-

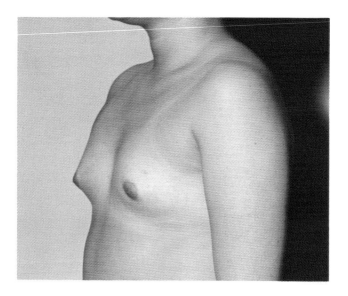

Figure 12-1. Small breasts (case 30) in patient 17 years of age. Normal breast development is not essential for the occurrence of galactorrhea.

ally discontinued in November, 1971. For three or four years she had noted limited vision and blurring while driving. Because of progressive visual loss, roentgenograms of the skull were made in February, 1972, and showed evidence of an enlarged sella. Galactorrhea had been present about three to four months.

When she presented at this clinic, physical examination revealed obesity, acanthosis nigricans, secretions from both breasts on expression and mild bitemporal field defects. Roentgenograms of the skull showed evidence of a huge, partially destroyed sella. Laboratory evaluation revealed low levels of serum total and free thyroxin, TSH, estrogens and plasma corticosteroids.

On left frontal craniotomy, a chromophobe adenoma was removed. After operation 6,300 R were delivered to the sella. At her last examination in June, 1972, secretions could still be expressed from both breasts.

Comment.—This case is unusual in that galactorrhea was a relatively late manifestation of a pituitary tumor.

Case 30. — A 17-year-old girl was seen in August, 1963, because of primary amenorrhea and lack of breast development. In 1961, studies elsewhere showed normal bone age, sellar configuration and thyroid function. Endometrial biopsy produced only a few fragments of fibrous stroma. Further evaluation included normal 24-hour urinary 17-ketosteroids and low concentrations of FSH. A cyclic estrogen-progesterone combination produced scanty withdrawal bleeding between 1962 and 1963. A few days of spontaneous scanty flow occurred in June, 1963.

Examination revealed normal female distribution of hair with slight breast development and small darkened nipples. The uterus was infantile. Laboratory evaluations indicated normal concentrations of corticosteroid, pituitary gonadotropin and estrogen. Endometrial tissue was proliferative and a buccal smear was chromatin positive.

The patient returned for reevaluation in December, 1966. She had had no spontaneous menses and the breasts were poorly developed (Fig. 12-1). Libido was absent. On further questioning, she revealed a history of persistent secretion from the nipples since she was 13 years of age. Examination showed small but engorged, cystic breasts producing a white watery discharge on palpation. The vaginal estrogen effect was good, but the uterus was small. Roentgenograms revealed evidence of an intrasellar tumor. Visual fields were normal. Urinary corticosteroid, gonadotropin and estrogen levels remained normal. On review of roentgenograms of the skull from 1961 and 1962, evidence of minimal abnormalities of the sella was noted (Fig. 12-2). A course of radiation by linear accelerator was given.

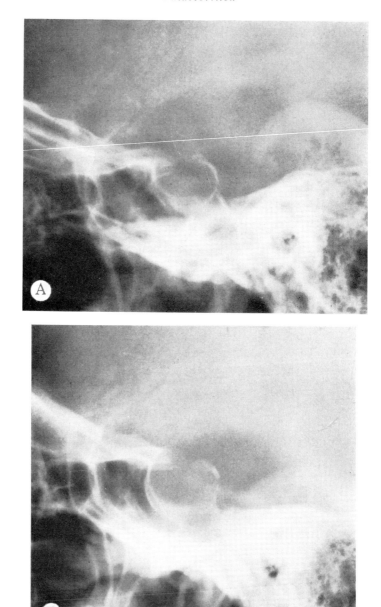

Figure 12-2. *A*—Cella (case 30) in 1961. *B*—Sella in same patient in 1966. Note enlargement.

In June, 1967, augmentation mammoplasty was performed. Secretions increased after operation, then continued at a diminished rate and were present at the time of her last examination in April, 1971. Cyclic hormone therapy continued to produce withdrawal bleeding but had no apparent effect on the galactorrhea.

Comment.—This case is another example of delayed diagnosis of a pituitary tumor in a patient with long-standing galactorrhea. Galactorrhea secondary to augmentation mammoplasty has been reported (95).

Case 31. — A 41-year-old housewife (G-VI, P-0, Ab-6) was first seen at the Mayo Clinic in February, 1965, complaining of diffuse myalgia. Menarche occurred at 13 years of age with subsequent episodes of hypomenorrhea and menometrorrhagia. Her first abortion in 1947 was followed by persistent bilateral, spontaneous lactation that continued through subsequent pregnancies. Secretion tended to be more profuse during menses and pregnancies. Menses failed to recur after her last spontaneous abortion in 1951; she remained amenorrheic until 1956, when menses returned spontaneously. The patient had always suffered from severe emotional problems.

Except for obesity and breast secretions no abnormality was apparent on physical examination. The patient expressed milky fluid in strong streams from both breasts. Fundi and visual fields were normal. The sella was slightly enlarged to the right. A mammogram showed fibrocystic changes.

Comment.—Only after 18 years of continuous lactation beginning in the postpartum period was evidence of a pituitary tumor finally discovered.

Case 32. — A 22-year old woman (G-0) entered the Mayo Clinic in January, 1967, for rhinoplasty. Breasts and sexual hair developed at 11 years of age and menarche occurred at 13 years. Menses were regular for six months with subsequent oligomenorrhea. Except for one spontaneous period in September, 1966, she had not menstruated for more than a year. Some breast secretion had been present for many years.

Results of physical examination were normal except for milky fluid expressed from each breast. Visual fields were normal but roentgenograms of the skull showed evidence of an expanding intrasellar tumor. A course of radiation therapy was given. Menses started in December, 1968, and continued regularly. Minimal galactorrhea persisted.

Comment.—The return of spontaneous menses after treatment for Forbes-Albright syndrome is distinctly unusual, but also is reported in the next two cases (case 33 and 34).

Case 33. — A 15-year-old girl presented in September, 1969, complaining of galactorrhea and oligomenorrhea. Menarche occurred at ten years of age with normal regular menses until the year before her admission to this clinic when she had only three scanty periods. Breast fullness had developed with increasingly profuse milky secretions over the preceding year. She had gained 23 kg over the past two years. For one year she had had occasional generalized throbbing headaches.

Significant findings on examination were generalized obesity and engorged breasts from which milky fluid could easily be expressed. Visual fields were normal. Roentgenograms of the head showed evidence of expansion of the sella into the sphenoid. A course of radiation was administered. In November, 1970, menses resumed spontaneously and recurred every other month thereafter. Galactorrhea had continued to the last follow-up in April, 1972.

Case 34. — A 21-year-old woman (G-0) presented in January, 1969, with amenorrhea. Sexual hair and breasts developed at 11 years of age. Menarche occurred at 12 years of age and menses were normal until she was 18, when they became irregular. Amenorrhea had been present since July, 1968. The breasts had not changed in size but secretions had been noted for about two years. She had had minor headaches two or three times a week since the summer of 1968. There was no history of drug intake or excessive mammary manipulation.

Examination was normal except for expression of a few drops of milk from each nipple. The visual fields were normal. Roentgenograms of the sella were without evidence of abnormality but tomograms revealed thinning of the sellar floor; 4,000 R were delivered to the sella. After radiation treatment, cyclic hormone therapy was started with subsequent withdrawal bleeding. She had no further headaches. Ingestion of hormones was discontinued in July, 1970. She subsequently had normal spontaneous menses and became pregnant in September, 1971, without specific therapy. Lactation ceased with the onset of pregnancy. In May, 1972, she gave birth to a normal infant which she did not nurse. Menses resumed spontaneously, but breast secretions did not persist after the immediate postpartum period.

Comment.—Return of menses and subsequent pregnancy are unusual after radiation therapy for an intrasellar tumor.

Case 35. — A 19-year-old college co-ed (G-0) complained of headaches and amenorrhea on admission to the Mayo Clinic in November, 1970. Onset of menses at ten years of age was followed by regular periods. She had had recurrent left temporal headaches for five years. Menses had become irregular four years previously with complete amenorrhea for the preceding three years. Cyclic hormones produced withdrawal bleeding. Intermittently, for three years, she had noted secretions from the breasts.

Results of physical examination were normal except for a small uterus and breast secretions on expression. Visual fields were normal but roentgenograms of the head revealed a parasellar and intrasellar tumor. Radiation therapy was given. Galactorrhea subsequently diminished somewhat, but amenorrhea persisted.

Case 36. — A 22-year-old married college student (G-0) presented at the Mayo Clinic in May, 1972, complaining of irregular menses since January, 1971.

Menses had been normal to August, 1970, when she began taking oral contraceptives. These were discontinued in January, 1971, but she experienced no spontaneous menses. Hormone injections were given on three occasions and withdrawal bleeding occurred twice. She had not had hot flashes. During the previous year she had noted occasional frontal headaches and had gained 7 kg. Galactorrhea had been present for approximately six months.

Physical examination was normal except for full breasts from which milky secretions were readily expressed. Roentgenograms of the skull revealed demineralization of the sella floor. Tomograms of the sella and fractional encephalography confirmed the presence of an intrasellar tumor. Visual fields were normal. Urinary determinations for urinary estrogens, ketosteroids and ketogenic steroids and serum determinations of total thyroxin and FSH were within normal limits. Urinary pituitary gonadotropins and serum LH were low.

Radiation therapy was given to the sella. At the time of her last examination in August, 1972, breast secretions were still present. Menses had not resumed.

Case 37. — A 47-year-old woman (G-III, P-3) presented at the Mayo Clinic in October, 1971, complaining of morning headaches. She had been referred by her physician for evaluation of probable renovascular hypertension. Menses had occurred at 13 years of age. She had a history of frequent premenstrual left frontotemporal headaches. She had had three uncomplicated pregnancies and deliveries 19, 20 and 21 years previously. Menses remained normal and regular after delivery, occurring every 26 days with five days' flow. She nursed her infants successfully after each delivery with cessation of lactation on weaning.

Galactorrhea was first noted for one month in 1966 with a milky discharge from both breasts, but only on manual expression. This ceased spontaneously. In January, 1968, her headaches increased in frequency and severity. Medical evaluation at that time revealed severe hypertension. Treatment with methyldopa (250 mg four times daily) was started; the amount was increased to 500 mg three times daily and hydrochlorothiazide (HydroDIURIL®), hydralazine (Apresoline®), and diazepam (Valium) were added. She had never taken contraceptive pills. By December, 1968, galactorrhea recurred spontaneously and persisted until her admission.

Physical examination revealed galactorrhea affecting both breasts on manual expression. Except for the presence of hypertension, results of the remainder of the examination, including a detailed neurologic evaluation, were negative. Roentgenograms of the skull showed evidence of an enlarged sella. Examinations of the fundus and visual fields gave negative results.

The patient eventually underwent surgical treatment for renovascular hypertension, but it was elected not to treat the pituitary lesion in view of the paucity of symptoms and related findings at that time. Close follow-up of the patient's condition and repeated sellar examinations were planned. Persistent lactation was noted at the time of her most recent visit in July, 1972.

Comment.—Galactorrhea associated with the use of methyldopa has been reported (68, 172, 229). This case emphasizes the importance of searching for a possible intrasellar or suprasellar tumor even though the patient is using a drug known to be associated with galactorrhea.

Case 38. — A 21-year-old nulliparous woman was seen at the Mayo Clinic in October, 1969, for evaluation of severe frontal headaches of four months' duration. Menarche occurred at 12 years of age with normal menses to the summer of 1966, when she became amenorrheic. Subsequently, only withdrawal bleeding could be induced. In the summer of 1967, galactorrhea not previously noted by the patient was found on examination. From that time, she continued to be able to express small amounts of milk from both breasts.

Serial roentgenograms of the skull from April, 1967, to August, 1969, did not show evidence of abnormality. She had gained 18 kg since the summer of 1968.

On physical examination obesity was noted and milky fluid was expressed from each breast. Evidence of ballooning of the sella was found on roentgenograms of the skull. Radiation therapy was instituted with relief of headaches, but with continued amenorrhea and and somewhat diminished galactorrhea at a two-year follow-up.

Comment.—Repeated examinations over a number of years may be necessary to rule out the presence of sellar or suprasellar tumors in patients with amenorrhea and galactorrhea.

Case 39. — A 35-year-old woman (G-I, P-1) presented in October, 1969, complaining of galactorrhea and amenorrhea. Menarche occurred at 15 years of age. At age 18, she became amenorrheic for several months. Menses resumed after treatment with thyroid hormone. From 1952 to 1960, she was unable to become pregnant although contraceptives were not used. In 1955, there was spontaneous onset of galactorrhea with menstrual irregularity. Hormonal therapy was not beneficial. Galactorrhea ceased spontaneously in 1957. After her pregnancy in 1960, she nursed the infant for only one month, but secretions continued. Menses returned six weeks after delivery but ceased four months later. She had a gradual loss of libido and gained 28 kg. She complained of frequent headaches.

Results of physical examination were normal except for milky secretions from both breasts, which were large. Laboratory evaluation was unremarkable except for low normal urinary gonadotropins and urinary estrogen of 0 RU/24 hours. Roentgenograms of the skull showed some evidence of demineralization of the dorsum sella.

Comment.—This case may well be an example of the previously reported evolution through the classic syndromes (142, 244). (See Chapter 6.)

Stress-Associated Galactorrhea

Case 40. — A 50-year-old housewife (G-II, P-2) presented at the Mayo Clinic in April, 1972, complaining of abdominal distress. Menarche had occurred at age 13. She had experienced regular menses every 28 to 30 days with moderate flow. She had had normal pregnancies and deliveries. Nineteen years previously she had nursed her last child for seven months, but lactation had continued for six additional months before ceasing spontaneously. For the preceding several years she had experienced menometrorrhagia. She had not taken either tranquilizers or oral contraceptives.

Findings were consistent with chronic cholecystitis. During her clinic stay she underwent cholecystectomy as well as dilatation and curettage without incident. Within the immediate postoperative period she noted bilateral milky secretions while showering. These secretions rapidly diminished particularly after menses in May, 1972. By July, 1972, secretion had ceased spontaneously. Laboratory examinations, including roentgenograms of the skull and visual fields, showed no evidence of abnormality.

Comment.—This patient manifested an abnormality of her lactation mechanisms by prolongation of physiologic lactation 19 years prior to an episode of stress-induced galactorrhea.

Idiopathic Galactorrhea

Case 41. — A 29-year-old woman (G-III, P-3) came to the Mayo Clinic in September, 1971, for reevaluation after surgical treatment for right hydronephrosis. She related that she had been able to express milky secretions from both breasts since the birth of her second child in August, 1965. After the birth of her first child in April, 1961, she had required two courses of hormone pills over a period of several weeks to stop lactation. After her delivery in August, 1965, she had nursed her infant for six or seven months and had experienced irregular menses before weaning her child. Menses became regular but breast secretions continued. She nursed her third child, born in May, 1969, for five months. Menses returned but breast secretions continued after weaning. Although flow was not spontaneous, she was always able to express secretions when she examined her breasts once a month. She had not taken contraceptives, tranquilizers or other long-term medication.

Except for the presence of bilateral galactorrhea physical examination was unremarkable. Results of routine laboratory tests were normal. Roentgenograms of the skull showed no evidence of abnormality.

Comment.—The absence of menstrual disturbance makes the presence of a serious underlying disorder less likely, but is not sufficient reason to neglect close follow-up in such a patient.

CHAPTER 13

CONCLUSIONS

THE UNPREDICTABLE OCCURRENCE of galactorrhea reflects our incomplete understanding of lactation physiology. In most cases studied, galactorrhea is associated with inappropriately high production of prolactin in a setting conducive to production of milk. Within the last few years, newer techniques, including prolactin assays, have enabled us to go slightly beyond clinical observation in explaining the factors involved in the normal and the abnormal production of milk.

Though the recently described provocative tests hold great promise, delineation of the more benign causes of abnormal lactation from serious organic disease is frequently based on prolonged clinical observation. In the 24 female patients in our series who had galactorrhea associated with a tumor in or near the sella turcica, the interval between the onset of galactorrhea and the discovery of the presence of tumor was as long as 18 years (Table 13-I). Eleven patients were nulliparous. In nine others, galactorrhea began in the postpartum period, while four patients had been pregnant previously but the onset of galactor-

TABLE 13-I.
TIME FROM ONSET OF GALACTORRHEA TO DIAGNOSIS OF
INTRACRANIAL TUMOR IN 23 FEMALE PATIENTS

	Number of patients	Time, years	
		Average	Range
Forbes-Albright syndrome*	15	5	3/12-18
Acromegaly	3	4	0-11
Craniopharyngioma	3	3	1 6/12-5
Pinealoma	1	3	. . .
Astrocytoma	1	1	. . .

*One patient, who had had galactorrhea for "many years", is not included in this series.

83

rhea was unrelated to parturition (Table 13-II). Of these 24 patients, eight had an initial history compatible with Del Castillo
syndrome, eight with Chiari-Frommel syndrome and seven with
other benign galactorrhea-associated conditions. In only one patient was strong evidence for tumor discovered before galactorrhea
was noted (Table 13-III). A history of oral contraceptive or psychotropic drug ingestion associated with the onset of galactorrhea
was no assurance that an underlying organic lesion did not exist.

TABLE 13-II.
PARITY OF 24 FEMALE PATIENTS HAVING GALACTORRHEA
ASSOCIATED WITH INTRACRANIAL TUMOR

| | Parous | | |
	Nonpostpartum	Postpartum	Nulliparous
Forbes-Albright syndrome	2	4	10
Acromegaly	1	2	...
Craniopharyngioma	1	2	...
Pinealoma	...	1	...
Astrocytoma	...	...	1

Although the management of galactorrhea, as a symptom, has
not been particularly successful, fortunately it is rarely a distress-
ing problem. The newer drugs hold some promise—levodopa, the
newer ergot preparations for treatment of amenorrhea and galactorrhea, and clomiphene for induction of pregnancy in selected
cases.

TABLE 13-III.
INITIAL CLINICAL PRESENTATION IN 24 FEMALE PATIENTS HAVING
GALACTORRHEA ASSOCIATED WITH INTRACRANIAL TUMOR

Del Castillo syndrome	8
Chiari-Frommel syndrome	8
Postcontraceptive pill	2
Primary amenorrhea	2
Del Castillo-Chiari-Frommel evolution	1
Idiopathic postpartum galactorrhea	1
Acromegaly	1
Methyldopa-induced	1

REFERENCES

1. Adams, F.: *The Genuine Works of Hippocrates.* Baltimore, The Williams & Wilkins Co., 1939, p. 318.
2. Aguilar, R. F.: Chiari Frommel syndrome: report of a case. *Am Pract Dig Treat, 11:* 509, 1960.
3. Ahumada, J. C., and Del Castillo, E. B.: Sobre un caso de galactorrea y amenorrea. *Bol Soc Obstet Ginec Buenos Aires, 11:* 64, 1932.
4. Albores Culebro, C.: Un caso de ginecomastia o androgalactozemia. *Torreon Med, 1:* 80, 1946.
5. Anderson, M. S., Erickson, L. S., and Luse, S. A.: Chiari-Frommel syndrome associated with a craniopharyngioma. *Neurology (Minneap.), 12:* 583, 1962.
6. Arenas Adarve, M., Durán Martínez, I., Charco Entrena, F., and Higuera Rojas, J.: Un caso de galactorrea e hipotiroidismo. *Rev Clin Esp, 86:* 229, 1962.
7. Argonz, J., and Del Castillo, E. B.: A syndrome characterized by estrogenic insufficiency, galactorrhea and decreased urinary gonadotropin. *J Clin Endocrinol Metab, 13:* 79, 1953.
8. Aruffo, R. N.: Lactation as a denial of separation. *Psychoanal Q, 40:* 100, 1971.
9. Ashkar, P. A.: Chiari's syndrome: report of a case. *J Obstet Gynaecol Br Commonw, 57:* 78, 1950.
10. Atkinson, F. R. B.: *Acromegaly.* London, John Bale, Sons & Danielsson, Ltd., 1932.
11. Aufses, A. H.: Abnormal lactation following radical mastectomy. *NY State J Med, 55:* 1914, 1955.
12. Averill, R. L. W.: The hypothalamus and lactation. *Br Med Bull, 22:* 261, 1966.
13. Ayd, F. J., Jr.: Thorazine and Serpasil treatment of private neuropsychiatric patients. *Am J Psychiatry, 113:* 16, 1956.
14. Bab, H.: Akromegalie und Ovarialtherapie. *Zentralbl Gynaekol, 38:* 26, 1914.
15. Barker, M., and Barker, A.: Late lactation. *Br Med J, 1:* 1365, 1960.
16. Barnes, A. B.: Current concepts: diagnosis and treatment of abnormal breast secretions. *N Engl J Med, 275:* 1184, 1966.
17. Bayliss, P. F. C., and van't Hoff, W.: Amenorrhoea and galactorrohea associated with hypothroidism. *Lancet, 2:* 1399, 1969.

18. Bearzi, V. L., Golijow, B., and Pintado, O. A.: Galactorrea postcastracion. *Prensa Med Argent, 45:* 2673, 1958.
19. Bellut, H.: Galaktorrhoe nach Pneumencephalographie. *Med Klin, 47:* 1314, 1952.
20. Benjamin, F., Casper, D. J., and Kolodny, H. H.: Immunoreactive human growth hormone in conditions associated with galactorrhea. *Obstet Gynecol, 34:* 34, 1969.
21. Bercovici, B., and Ehrenfeld, E. N.: Non-puerperal galactorrhoea. *J Obstet Gynaecol Br Commonw, 70:* 295, 1963.
22. Berger, R. L., Joison, J., and Braverman, L. E.: Lactation after incision on the thoracic cage. *N Engl J Med, 274:* 1493, 1966.
23. Bittorf, A.: Nebennierentumor und Geschlechtsdrüsenausfall beim Manne. *Berl Klin Wochnschr, 56:* 776, 1919.
24. Bivin, G. D., and Klinger, M. P.: *Pseudocyesis.* Bloomington, Indiana, The Principia Press, Inc., 1937, p. 41.
25. Blum, D. M., and Smythe, A. M.: Abnormal lactation. *J Iowa Med Soc, 20:* 206, 1930.
26. Bolognese, R. J., Piver, M. S., and Feldman, J. D.: Galactorrhea and abnormal menses associated with a long-acting progesterone. *JAMA, 199:* 42, 1967.
27. Bowers, C. Y., Friesen, H. G., Hwang, P., Guyda, H. J., and Folkers, K.: Prolactin and thyrotropin release in man by synthetic pyroglutamyl-histidyl-prolinamide. *Biochem Biophys Res Commun, 45:* 1033, 1971.
28. Braga, C., Jones, J., Mendenhall, H., and Goldfien, A.: Evidence for independent growth and lactogenic principles in man. *Clin Res, 14:* 130, 1966.
29. Brazeau, P., Vale, W., Burgus, R., Ling, N., Butcher, M., Rivier, J., and Guillemin, R.: Hypothalamic polypeptide that inhibits the secretion of immunoreactive pituitary growth hormone. *Science, 179:* 77, 1973.
30. Briehl, W., and Kulka, E. W.: Lactation in a virgin. *Psychoanal Q, 4:* 484, 1935.
31. Brown, D. M., Jenness, R., and Ulstrom, R. A.: A study of the composition of milk from a patient with hypothyroidism and galactorrhea. *J Clin Endocrinol Metab, 25:* 1225, 1965.
32. Canfield, C. J., and Bates, R. W.: Nonpuerperal galactorrhea. *N Engl J Med, 273:* 897, 1965.
33. Cartlidge, N. E. F., and Hudgson, P.: Inappropriate lactation (letter to the editor). *Br Med J, 3:* 529, 1969.
34. Chard, T.: The Chiari-Frommel syndrome: an experiment of nature. *J Obstet Gynaecol Br Commonw, 71:* 624, 1964.
35. Chiari, J. B. V. L., Braun, C., and Spaeth, J.: *Klinik der Geburtshilfe und Gynäkologie.* Erlangen, F. Enke, 1855, p. 375.

36. Chrambach, A., Bridson, W. E., and Turkington, R. W.: Human prolactin: identification and physical characterization of the biologically active hormone by polyacrylamide gel electrophoresis. *Biochem Biophys Res Commun, 43:* 1296, 1971.

37. Christiansen, E. G.: A case of Chiari-Frommel's syndrome. *Acta Endocrinol (Kbh), 24:* 407, 1957.

38. Clinicopathologic Conference: Non-puerperal galactorrhea, amenorrhea and visual loss. *Am J Med, 33:* 591, 1962.

39. Cohen, A.: Amenorrhoea and prolonged lactation, including a further report of the Chiari-Frommel syndrome. *Australas Ann Med, 8:* 77, 1959.

40. Cohen, I. M.: Complications of chlorpromazine therapy. *Am J Psychiatry, 113:* 115, 1956.

41. Cooke, J. V.: Chorio-epithelioma of the testicle. *Johns Hopkins Med J, 26:* 215, 1915.

42. Coppedge, R. L., and Segaloff, A.: Urinary prolactin excretion in man. *J Clin Endocrinol Metab, 11:* 465, 1951.

43. Costin, G., Kogut, M. D., Kershnar, A. K., and Turkington, R. W.: Plasma prolactin levels in juvenile hypothyroidism and precocious puberty (abstract). *Pediatr Res, 6:* 351, 1972.

44. Cramer, B.: Delusion of pregnancy in a girl with drug-induced lactation. *Am J Psychiatry, 127:* 960, 1971.

45. Cross, B. A., and Harris, G. W.: The role of the neurohypophysis in the milk-ejection reflex. *J Endocrinol, 8:* 148, 1952.

46. Cushing, H.: "Dyspituitarism": twenty years later, with special consideration of the pituitary adenomas. *Arch Intern Med, 51:* 487, 1933.

47. Dadey, J. L., and Hurxthal, L. M.: Abnormal lactation: report of a case with amenorrhea and diabetes insipidus. *Lahey Clin Found Bull, 10:* 166, 1957.

48. Danowski, T. S.: *Clinical Endocrinology.* Vol. 1. Baltimore, The Williams & Wilkins Company, 1962, p. 460.

49. Davidoff, L. M.: Studies in acromegaly. III. The anamnesis and symptomatology in one hundred cases. *Endocrinology, 10:* 461, 1926.

50. Davidson, J. M., Contopoulos, A. N., and Ganong, W. F.: Decreased gonadotrophic hormone content of the anterior pituitary gland in dogs with hypothalamic lesions. *Endocrinology, 66:* 735, 1960.

51. Del Castillo, E. B., and Lanari, A.: Sindrome caracterizado por crecimiento exagerado, amenorea y galactorrea y acromegalia. *Semana Med, 1:* 1905, 1933.

52. Del Pozo, E., and Audibert, A.: Ergot treatment of nonpuerperal galactorrhea (letter to the editor). *N Engl J Med, 287:* 723, 1972.

53. Del Pozo, E., Brun del Re, R., Varga, L., and Friesen, H.: The inhibition of prolactin secretion in man by CB-154 (2-Br-α-ergocryptine). *J Clin Endocrinol Metab, 35:* 768, 1972.

54. *Dorland's Illustrated Medical Dictionary.* 24th Ed., Philadelphia, W. B. Saunders Company, 1965, p. 593.

55. Dormer, A. E., and Watts, R. W. E.: Galactorrhoea. *Br Med J, 1:* 609, 1962.

56. Dowling, J. T., Richards, J. B., Freinkel, N., and Ingbar, S. H.: Nonpuerperal galactorrhea: eleven cases without enlargement of the sella turcica. *Arch Intern Med, 107:* 885, 1961.

57. Dugger, G. S., Van Wyk, J. J., and Newsome, J. F.: The effect of pituitary-stalk section on thyroid function and gonadotropic-hormone excretion in women with mammary carcinoma. *J Neurosurg, 19:* 589, 1962.

58. Edwards, C. R. W., Forsyth, I. A., and Besser, G. M.: Amenorrhoea, galactorrhoea, and primary hypothyroidism with high circulating levels of prolactin. *Br Med J, 3:* 462, 1971.

59. Ehni, G., and Eckles, N. E.: Interruption of the pituitary stalk in the patient with mammary cancer. *J Neurosurg, 16:* 628, 1959.

60. Enzmann, F., Bøler, J., Folkers, K., Bowers, C. Y., and Schally, A. V.: Structure and synthesis of the thyrotropin-releasing hormone. *J Med Chem, 14:* 469, 1971.

61. Everett, N. B., and Baker, B. L.: The distribution of cell types in the anterior hypophysis during late pregnancy and lactation. *Endocrinology, 37:* 83, 1945.

62. Fazio, F.: Sopra un caso di acromegalia. *Riforma Med, 2:* 399, 1896.

63. Ferguson, K. A., and Wallace, A. L. C.: The characterization of pituitary hormones by starch gel electrophoresis. *Recent Progr Horm Res, 19:* 1, 1963.

64. Finn, J. E., and Mount, L. A.: Galactorrhea in males with tumors in the region of the pituitary gland. *J Neurosurg, 35:* 723, 1971.

65. Forbes, A. P., Henneman, P. H., Griswold, G. C., and Albright, F.: Syndrome characterized by galactorrhea, amenorrhea and low urinary FSH: comparison with acromegaly and normal lactation. *J Clin Endocrinol Metab, 14:* 265, 1954.

66. Forsyth, I. A., Besser, G. M., Edwards, C. R. W., Francis, L., and Myres, R. P.: Plasma prolactin activity in inappropriate lactation. *Br Med J, 3:* 225, 1971.

67. Foss, G. L., and Short, D.: Abnormal lactation. *J Obstet Gynaecol Br Commonw, 58:* 35, 1951.

68. Frantz, A. G., and Kleinberg, D. L.: Prolactin: evidence that it is separate from growth hormone in human blood. *Science, 170:* 745, 1970.

69. Friedman, S., and Goldfien, A.: Amenorrhea and galactorrhea following oral contraceptive therapy. *JAMA, 210:* 1888, 1969.

70. Friedman, S., and Goldfien, A.: Breast secretions in normal women. *Am J Obstet Gynecol, 104:* 846, 1969.

71. Friesen, H., Guyda, H., Hwang, P., Tyson, J. E., and Barbeau, A.:

Functional evaluation of prolactin secretion: a guide to therapy. *J Clin Invest, 51:* 706, 1972.

72. Friesen, H., Webster, B. R., Hwang, P., Guyda, H., Munro, R. E., and Read, L.: Prolactin synthesis and secretion in a patient with the Forbes Albright syndrome. *J Clin Endocrinol Metab, 34:* 192, 1972.

73. Friesen, H. G.: Serum prolactin concentrations. Read at the meeting of Advances in Clinical Endocrinology, Boston, March 7, 1972.

74. Friesen, H. G.: Prolactin: its physiologic role and therapeutic potential. *Hosp Pract, 7:* 123, 1972.

75. Frommel, R.: Ueber puerperale Atrophie des Uterus. *Z Geburtshilfe Gynaekol, 7:* 305, 1882.

76. Futterweit, W., and Goodsell, C. H.: Galactorrhea in primary hypothyroidism: report of two cases and review of the literature. *Mt. Sinai J Med NY, 37:* 584, 1970.

77. Gentile, L. A.: Galactorrhea following extirpation of the uterus and both ovaries. *NY State J Med, 60:* 3468, 1960.

78. Gilbert, B.: Persistent lactation with a note on Chiari and Frommel's disease. *Br Med J, 2:* 305, 1941.

79. Gordon, D. A., Hill, F. M., and Ezrin, C.: Acromegaly: a review of 100 cases. *Can Med Assoc J, 87:* 1106, 1962.

80. Gordon, D. L., and Cicurel, N. J.: Galactorrhea. *Chic Med Sch Q, 28:* 133, 1969.

81. Greenblatt, R. B., Carmona, N., and Hagler, W. S.: Chiari-Frommel syndrome: a syndrome characterized by galactorrhea, amenorrhea, and pituitary dysfunction: report of two cases. *Obstet Gynecol, 7:* 165, 1956.

82. Greenblatt, R. B., and Mahesh, V. B.: The ovary: induction of ovulation with clomiphene citrate. *Yearbook Endocrinol,* 1965, p. 248.

83. Greenway, P. J.: Artificially induced lactation in humans. *East Afr Med J, 13:* 346, 1937.

84. Gregg, W. I.: Galactorrhea after contraceptive hormones. *N Engl J Med, 274:* 1432, 1966.

85. Grimm, E. G.: Non-puerperal galactorrhea with case reports. *Q Bull Northwestern Univ Med Sch, 29:* 350, 1955.

86. Groseclose, E. S.: Chiari-Frommel syndrome: a review with report of a case. *Obstet Gynecol, 21:* 372, 1963.

87. Grossman, S., Buchberg, A. S., Brecher, E., and Hallinger, L. M.: Idiopathic lactation following thoracoplasty. *J Clin Endocrinol Metab, 10:* 729, 1950.

88. Grosvenor, C. E.: Effect of nursing and stress upon prolactin-inhibiting activity of the rat hypothalamus. *Endocrinology, 77:* 1037, 1965.

89. Grosvenor, C. E., McCann, S. M., and Nallar, R.: Inhibition of nursing-induced and stress-induced fall in pituitary prolactin concentra-

tion in lactating rats by injection of acid extracts of bovine hypothalamus. *Endocrinology, 76:* 883, 1965.

90. Guinet, P., Putelat, R., Tommasi, M., Descours, C., and Franchet, G.: Un cas de craniopharyngiome avec galactorrhée et aménorrhée. *Ann Endocrinol (Paris), 22:* 385, 1961.

91. Gumpel, R. C.: Pituitary tumor, postpartum amenorrhea, and galactorrhea, with comment on Chiari-Frommel syndrome. *NY State J Med, 60:* 3304, 1960.

92. Guyda, H., Hwang, P., and Friesen, H.: Immunologic evidence for monkey and human prolactin (MPr and HPr). *J Clin Endocrinol Metab, 32:* 120, 1971.

93. Haenel, H.: Ein Fall von dauernder Milchsekretion beim Manne. *Munch Med Wochenschr, 1:* 261, 1928.

94. Hamwi, G. J., Skillman, T. G., and Tufts, K. C., Jr.: Acromegaly. *Am J Med, 29:* 690, 1960.

95. Hartley, J. H., Jr., and Schatten, W. E.: Postoperative complication of lactation after augmentation mammaplasty. *Plast Reconstr Surg, 47:* 150, 1971.

96. Haskins, A. L., Moszkowski, E. F., and Cohen, H.: Chiari-Frommel syndrome: medroxyprogesterone acetate therapy. *Am J Obstet Gynecol, 88:* 667, 1964.

97. Haun, C. K., and Sawyer, C. H.: Initiation of lactation in rabbits following placement of hypothalamic lesions. *Endocrinology, 67:* 270, 1960.

98. Haun, C. K., and Sawyer, C. H.: The role of the hypothalamus in initiation of milk secretion. *Acta Endocrinol (Kbh.), 38:* 99, 1961.

99. Herlant, M., Laine, E., Fossati, P., and Linquette, M.: Syndrome aménorrhée-galactorrhée par adénome hypophysaire à cellules à prolactine. *Ann Endocrinol (Paris), 26:* 65, 1965.

100. Herlant, M., Linquette, M., Laine, E., Fossati, P., May, J.-P., and Lefebvre, J.: Adénome hypophysaire à cellules thyréotropes, avec syndrome aménorrhée-galactorrhée, chez une malade parteuse d'un myxoedeme congénital par ectopie thyroïdienne. *Ann Endocrinol (Paris), 27:* 181, 1966.

101. Herlant, M., and Pasteels, J. L.: Histophysiology of human anterior pituitary, in Methods and Achievements in Experimental Pathology. In Bajusz, E., and Jasmin, G. (Ed.), Year Book Medical Publishers, Inc., Chicago, 1966, p. 250.

102. Heuser, G., Batzdorf, U., Bentson, J. R., Blank, N., Dashe, A. M., Hepler, R. S., Rand, R. W., Roth, N. H., Rubenstein, M. K., Schechter, J., and Simmer, H. H.: Trends in clinical neuroendocrinology. *Ann Intern Med, 73:* 783, 1970.

103. Hooper, J. H., Jr., Welch, V. C., and Shackelford, R. T.: Abnormal

lactation associated with tranquilizing drug therapy. *JAMA, 178:* 506, 1961.

104. Hunt, A. B.: Postpartum amenorrhea. *Obstet Gynecol, 1:* 522, 1953.

105. Hurxthal, L. M., Hare, H. F., Horrax, G., and Poppen, J. L.: The treatment of acromegaly. *J Clin Endocrinol Metab, 9:* 126, 1949.

106. Hwang, P., Friesen, H., Hardy, J., and Wilansky, D.: Biosynthesis of human growth hormone and prolactin by normal pituitary glands and pituitary adenomas. *J Clin Endocrinol Metab, 33:* 1, 1971.

107. Hwang, P., Guyda, H., and Friesen, H.: A radioimmunoassay for human prolactin. *Proc Natl Acad Sci USA, 68:* 1902, 1971.

108. Ioanitiu, D., Stoica, T., Klepsch, I., Serban, A., Esanu, C., Stroe, E., and Ipsas, I.: Pituitary tumors with amenorrhea-galactorrhea syndrome. *Rev Roum Endocrinol, 7:* 63, 1970.

109. Jackson, W. P. U.: Post-thyroidectomy hypothyroidism, hypoparathyroidism, exophthalmos and galactorrhea with normal menstruation: metabolic response to probenecid. *J Clin Endocrinol Metab, 16:* 1245, 1956.

110. Jacobs, L. S., Snyder, P. J., Wilber, J. F., Utiger, R. D., and Daughaday, W. H.: Increased serum prolactin after administration of synthetic thyrotropin releasing hormone (TRH) in man. *J Clin Endocrinol Metab, 33:* 996, 1971.

111. Jaszmann, L.: The Chiari-Frommel syndrome. *J Obstet Gynaecol Br Commonw, 70:* 120, 1963.

112. Johnson, H. W., Poshyachinda, D., McCormick, G., and Hamblen, E. C.: Lactation with phenothiazine derivative (Temaril). *Am J Obstet Gynecol, 80:* 124, 1960.

113. Jull, J. W., Henderson, W. R., and Short, R. V.: Persistent lactation associated with high oestrogen excretion and cystic ovaries in a woman with a previous history of a chromophobe adenoma of the pituitary. *J Reprod Fertil, 7:* 367, 1964.

114. Kaiser, I. H.: Pregnancy following clomiphene-induced ovulation in Chiari-Frommel syndrome. *Am J Obstet Gynecol, 87:* 149, 1963.

115. Kamberi, I. A., Mical, R. S., and Porter, J. C.: Hypophysial portal vessel infusion: *in vivo* demonstration of LRF, FRF, and PIF in pituitary stalk plasma. *Endocrinology, 89:* 1042, 1971.

116. Kaplan, S. L., Grumbach, M. M., Friesen, H. G., and Costom, B. H.: Thyrotropin-releasing factor (TRF) effect on secretion of human pituitary prolactin and thyrotropin in children and in idiopathic hypopituitary dwarfism: further evidence for hypophysiotropic hormone deficiencies. *J Clin Endocrinol Metab, 35:* 825, 1972.

117. Khazan, N., Primo, C., Danon, A., Assael, M., Sulman, F. G., and Winnik, H. Z.: The mammotropic effect of tranquilizing drugs. *Arch Int Pharmacodyn Ther, 136:* 291, 1962.

118. Kinch, R. A. H., Plunkett, E. R., and Devlin, M. C.: Postpartum amen-

orrhea-galactorrhea of hypothyroidism. *Am J Obstet Gynecol, 105:* 766, 1969.

119. Kinross-Wright, V.: Complications of chlorpromazine treatment. *Dis Nerv Syst, 16:* 114, 1955.

120. Klein, J. J., Segal, R. L., and Warner, R. R. P.: Galactorrhea due to imipramine: report of a case. *N Engl J Med, 271:* 510, 1964.

121. Kleinberg, D. L., Noel, G. L., and Frantz, A. G.: Chlorpromazine stimulation and L-dopa suppression of plasma prolactin in man. *J Clin Endocrinol Metab, 33:* 873, 1971.

122. Kneeland: Prolonged secretion of milk. *Am J Med Sci, 23:* 110, 1852.

123. Knott, J.: Abnormal lactation: in the virgin; in the old woman; in the male; in the newborn of either sex ("witches milk"). *Am Med, 13:* 373, 1907.

124. Krestin, D.: Spontaneous lactation associated with enlargement of the pituitary: with report of 2 cases. *Lancet, 1:* 928, 1932.

125. Lampe, W. T., II: Lactation following psychotropic agents. *Metabolism, 16:* 257, 1967.

126. Lavrič, M. V.: Galactorrhea and amenorrhea with polycystic ovaries: Del Castillo syndrome or polycystic ovarian syndrome. *Am J Obstet Gynecol, 104:* 814, 1969.

127. Lawrence, A. M., and Hagen, T. C.: Ergonovine therapy of nonpuerperal galactorrhea (letter to the editor). *N Engl J Med, 287:* 150, 1972.

128. Leis, H. P., and Pilnik, S.: Nipple discharge. *Hosp Med, 6:* 29, 1970.

129. Levin, M. E., Daughaday, W. H., and Levy, I.: Persistent lactation associated with pituitary tumor and hyperadrenal corticism: successfully treated with pituitary radiation. *Am J Med, 27:* 172, 1959.

130. Levine, H. J., Bergenstal, D. M., and Thomas, L. B.: Persistent lactation: endocrine and histologic studies in 5 cases. *Am J Med Sci, 243:* 67, 1962.

131. L'Hermite, M., Vanhaelst, L., Copinschi, G., Leclercq, R., Golstein, J., Bruno, O. D., and Robyn, C.: Prolactin release after injection of thyrotrophin-releasing hormone in man. *Lancet, 1:* 763, 1972.

132. Liggins, G. C., and Ibbertson, H. K.: A successful quintuplet pregnancy following treatment with human pituitary gonadotrophin. *Lancet, 1:* 114, 1966.

133. Linquette, M., Herlant, M., Laine, E., Fossati, P., and Dupont-Decompte, J.: Adénome à prolactine chez une jeune fille dont la mère était porteuse d' un adénome hypophysaire avec aménorrhée-galactorrhée. *Ann Endocrinol (Paris), 28:* 773, 1967.

134. Lippard, C. H.: The Chiari-Frommel syndrome. *Am J Obstet Gynecol, 82:* 724, 1961.

135. Lisser, H.: A case of adrenal cortical tumor in an adult male causing gynecomastia and lactation. *Endocrinology, 20:* 567, 1936.

136. Lodge, S.: An address on cases illustrating some intracranial conditions of general interest. *Br Med J, 1:* 592, 1912.

137. Loewenstein, J. E., Mariz, I. K., Peake, G. T., and Daughaday, W. H.: Prolactin bioassay by induction of N-acetyllactosamine synthetase in mouse mammary gland explants. *J Clin Endocrinol Metab, 33:* 217, 1971.

138. Loraine, J. A., Bell, E. T., Harkness, R. A., and Harrison, M. T.: The effect of clomiphene on hormone excretion in patients with galactorrhoea. *Acta Endocrinol (Kbh), 52:* 527, 1966.

139. Louros, N. C., Batrinos, M. L., Kaskarelis, D., Danezis, J., and Calliga, V.: Pituitary corticotrophin reserve and endocrine function in the syndrome of pitutitary adenoma with galactorrhea. *Int J Fertil, 12:* 368, 1967.

140. Lutterbeck, P. M., Pryor, J. S., Varga, L., and Wenner, L.: Treatment of non-puerperal galactorrhoea with an ergot alkaloid. *Br Med J, 3:* 228, 1971.

141. Lyons, W. R., and Dixon, J. S.: The physiology and chemistry of the mammotrophic hormone, in The Pituitary Gland. Vol 1, In Harris, G. W., and Donovan, B. T. (Ed.), University of California Press, Berkeley, 1966, p. 527.

142. Maas, J. M.: Amenorrhea-galactorrhea syndrome before, during, and after pregnancy. *Fertil Steril, 18:* 857, 1967.

143. Maguire: Acromegaly. *Br Med J, 1:* 535, 1909.

144. Maizels, G.: Spontaneous galactorrhoea in a virgin. *J Obstet Gynaecol Br Commonw, 74:* 933, 1967.

145. Malarkey, W. B., Jacobs, L. S., and Daughaday, W. H.: Levodopa suppression of prolactin in nonpuerperal galactorrhea. *N Engl J Med, 285:* 1160, 1971.

146. Marcovitz, S., and Friesen, H.: Regulation of prolactin secretion in man (abstract). *Clin Res, 19:* 773, 1971.

147. Marshall, W. K., and Leiberman, D. M.: A rare complication of chlorpromazine treatment. *Lancet, 1:* 162, 1956.

148. Matsuo, H., Baba, Y., Nair, R. M. G., Arimura, A., and Schally, A. V.: Structure of the porcine LH- and FSH- releasing hormone. I. The proposed amino acid sequence. *Biochem Biophys Res Commun, 43:* 1334, 1971.

149. McCann, S. M., and Friedman, H. M.: The effect of hypothalamic lesions on the secretion of luteotrophin. *Endocrinology, 67:* 597, 1960.

150. McCullagh, E. P., Alivisatos, J. G., and Schaffenburg, C .A.: Pituitary tumor with gynecomastia and lactation. *J Clin Endocrinol Metab, 16:* 397, 1956.

151. McDonald, C. J., and Lerner, A. B.: Atopic dermatitis and persistent lactation. *Arch Dermatol, 93:* 174, 1966.

152. Meites, J.: Effect of reserpine on prolactin content of rabbit pituitary. *Proc Soc Exp Biol Med, 97:* 742, 1958.
153. Meites, J.: Control of mammary growth and lactation, in Neuroendocrinology. Vol. 1, In Martini, L., and Ganong, W. F. (Ed.). New York, Academic Press, Inc., 1966, p. 676.
154. Meites, J., and Nicoll, C. S.: Adenohypophysis: prolactin. *Annu Rev Physiol, 28:* 57, 1966.
155. Melnyk, C. S., and Greer, M. A.: Functional pituitary tumor in an adult possibly secondary to long-standing myxedema. *J Clin Endocrinol Metab, 25:* 761, 1965.
156. Mendel, E. B.: Chiari-Frommel syndrome: an historical review with case report. *Am J Obstet Gynecol, 51:* 889, 1946.
157. Mendels, J.: Thioproperazine-induced lactation. *Am J Psychiatry, 121:* 190, 1964.
158. Monroe, J. H.: Abnormal lactation. *NC Med J, 18:* 283, 1957.
159. Moyer, J. H., Kinross-Wright, V., and Finney, R. M.: Chlorpromazine as a therapeutic agent in clinical medicine. *Arch Intern Med, 95:* 202, 1955.
160. Mulla, N. P.: Chiari-Frommel syndrome: report of a case. *Ohio State Med J, 61:* 358, 1965.
161. Nasr, H., Mozaffarian, G., Pensky, J., and Pearson, O. H.: Prolactin-secreting pituitary tumors in women. *J Clin Endocrinol Metab, 35:* 505, 1972.
162. Newton, M.: Human Lactation, in Milk: The Mammary Gland and Its Secretion. Vol. 1, In Kon, S. K., and Cowie, A. T. (Ed.), New York, Academic Press, Inc., 1961, p. 281.
163. Nikitovitch-Winer, M. B.: Effect of hypophysial stalk transection on luteotrophic hormone secretion in the rat. *Endocrinology, 77:* 658, 1965.
164. Noel, G. L., Suh, H. K., Stone, J. G., and Frantz, A. G.: Human prolactin and growth hormone release during surgery and other conditions of stress. *J Clin Endocrinol Metab, 35:* 840, 1972.
165. Nyirjesy, I.: Galactorrhea without amenorrhea. *Obstet Gynecol, 32:* 52, 1968.
166. Nyirjesy, I.: Ovarian morphology in amenorrhea-galactorrhea syndromes. *Am J Obstet Gynecol, 101:* 458, 1968.
167. Oestreich, R., and Slawyk: Riesenwuchs und zirbeldrüsen-Geschwulst. *Virchows Arch [Pathol Anat], 157:* 475, 1899.
168. Parkes Weber, F.: A note on the causation of gynaecomastia (mammary feminism). *Lancet, 1:* 1034, 1926.
169. Paterson, R., DePasquale, N., and Mann, S.: Pseudo-tumor cerebri. *Medicine (Baltimore), 40:* 85, 1961.
170. Peake, G. T., McKeel, D. W., Jarett, L., and Daughaday, W. H.: Ultrastructural histologic and hormonal characterization of a prolactin-

rich human pituitary tumor. *J Clin Endocrinol Metab, 29:* 1383, 1969.

171. Pernoll, M. L.: Diagnosis and treatment of galactorrhea. *Postgrad Med, 49:* 76, 1971.

172. Pettinger, W. A., Horwitz, D., and Sjoerdsma, A.: Lactation due to methyldopa. *Br Med J, 1:* 1460, 1963.

173. Phillips, A. F.: Late lactation. *Br Med J, 2:* 234, 1960.

174. Platt, R., and Sears, H. T. N.: Reserpine in severe hypertension. *Lancet, 1:* 401, 1956.

175. Potter, J. C.: Chiari's syndrome. *Am J Obstet Gynecol, 47:* 276, 1944.

176. Rankin, J. S., Goldfarb, A. F., and Rakoff, A. E.: Galactorrhea-amenorrhea syndromes: postpartum galactorrhea-amenorrhea in the absence of intracranial neoplasm. *Obstet Gynecol, 33:* 1, 1969.

177. Ravera, J. J., Tomalino, D., and Ganzalex, P.: Panhipituitarismo con galactorrhea secuela de meningitis tuberculosa curada. *Torax, 10:* 40, 1961.

178. Rees, W. D.: Lactation and ovarian cyst formation following treatment with amitriptyline. *Practitioner, 198:* 835, 1967.

179. Refetoff, S., Block, M. B., Ehrlich, E. N., and Friesen, H. G.: Chiari-Frommel syndrome in a patient with primary adrenocortical insufficiency: cure by glucocorticoid replacement. *N Engl J Med, 287:* 1326, 1972.

180. Relkin, R.: Neurologic pathways involved in lactation. *Dis Nerv Syst, 28:* 94, 1967.

181. Richardson, G. S.: Reflex lactation (thoracotomy) and reflex ovulation (intercostal block): case report, review of the literature, and discussion of mechanisms. *Obstet Gynecol Surv, 25:* 1021, 1970.

182. Riese, W.: Milchsekretion und Zurischenhirn. *Klin Wochenschr, 7:* 1954, 1928.

183. Rimoin, D. L., Holzman, G. B., Merimee, T. J., Rabinowitz, D., Barnes, A. C., Tyson, J. E. A., and McKusick, V. A.: Lactation in the absence of human growth hormone. *J Clin Endocrinol Metab, 28:* 1183, 1968.

184. Robinson, B.: Breast changes in the male and female with chlorpromazine or reserpine therapy. *Med J Aust, 2:* 239, 1957.

185. Rosen, S. W., and Gahres, E. E.: Nonpuerperal galactorrhea and the contraceptive pill. *Obstet Gynecol, 29:* 730, 1967.

186. Ross, F., and Nusynowitz, M. L.: A syndrome of primary hypothyroidism, amenorrhea and galactorrhea. *J Clin Endocrinol Metab, 28:* 591, 1968.

187. Roth, J., Gordon, P., and Bates, R. W.: Studies of growth hormone and prolactin in acromegaly. *Excerpta Medica International Congress Series No. 158,* 1968, p. 124.

188. Roth, O.: Auftreten von Milchsekretion bei einem an Akromegalie lei-denden Patienten. *Berl Klin Wochenschr, 1:* 305, 1918.

189. Roussy, G., de Gery, C., and Mosinger: A propos d'un cas de syringo-myélie avec galactorrhée et ileus postopératoire. *Rev Neurol (Paris), 1:* 521, 1932.

190. Russfield, A. B., Reiner, L., and Klaus, H.: The endocrine significance of hypophyseal tumors in man. *Am J Pathol, 32:* 1055, 1956.

191. Sachs, H. B.: Lactation after hysterectomy in a nulliparous woman. *Am J Obstet Gynecol, 78:* 204, 1959.

192. Sachson, R., Rosen, S. W., Cuatrecasas, P., Roth, J., and Frantz, A. G.: Prolactin stimulation by thyrotropin-releasing hormone in a pa-tient with isolated thyrotropin deficiency. *N Engl J Med, 287:* 972, 1972.

193. Salkin, D., and Davis, E. W.: Lactation following thoracoplasty and pneumonectomy. *J Thorac Cardiovasc Surg, 18:* 580, 1949.

194. Sassin, J. F., Frantz, A. G., Weitzman, E. D., and Kapen, S.: Human prolactin: 24-hour pattern with increased release during sleep. *Science, 177:* 1205, 1972.

195. Schachner, S. H.: Galactorrhea subsequent to contraceptive hormones. *N Engl J Med, 275:* 1138, 1966.

196. Schally, A. V., Arimura, A., and Kastin, A. J.: Hypothalamic regula-tory hormones: at least nine substances from the hypothalamus control the secretion of pituitary hormones. *Science, 179:* 341, 1973.

197. Schally, A. V., Kuroshima, A., Ishida, Y., Redding, T. W., and Bow-ers, C. Y.: The presence of prolactin inhibiting factor (PIF) in ex-tracts of beef, sheep and pig hypothalami. *Proc Soc Exp Biol Med, 118:* 350, 1965.

198. Schwartz, T. B.: *The Year Book of Endocrinology.* Chicago, Year Book Medical Publishers, Inc., 1971, p. 330.

199. Seifert, M. J.: Eccyesis, with prolonged lactation: case report, with a comprehensive review of the literature. *Internat Clin, 2:* 89, 1920.

200. Selye, H.: *Textbook of Endocrinology.* Montreal, University of Mon-treal, 1947, p. 291.

201. Sharp, E. A.: Historical review of a syndrome embracing uteroovarian atrophy with persistent lactation (Frommel's disease). *Am J Obstet Gynecol, 30:* 411, 1935.

202. Shearman, R. P.: Prolonged secondary amenorrhoea after oral con-traceptive therapy: natural and unnatural history. *Lancet, 2:* 64, 1971.

203. Shearman, R. P., and Turtle, J. R.: Secondary amenorrhea with inap-propriate lactation. *Am J Obstet Gynecol, 106:* 818, 1970.

204. Sheld, H. H.: Non-puerperal galactorrhea following hysterectomy. *Rocky Mt Med J, 65:* 57, 1968.

205. Sherwood, L. M.: Human prolactin. *N Engl J Med, 284:* 774, 1971.

206. Shevach, A. B., and Spellacy, W. N.: Galactorrhea and contraceptive practices. *Obstet Gynecol, 38:* 286, 1971.

207. Slome, C.: Nonpuerperal lactation in grandmothers. *J Pediatr, 49:* 550, 1956.

208. Somlyo, A. P., and Waye, J. D.: Abnormal lactation: report of a case induced by reserpine and a brief review of the subject. *Mt Sinai J Med NY, 27:* 5, 1960.

209. Spellacy, W. N., Carlson, K. L., and Schade, S. L.: Human growth hormone studies in patients with galactorrhea (Ahumada-Del Castillo syndrome). *Am J Obstet Gynecol, 100:* 84, 1968.

210. Staemmler, M.: Akromegalie und Lactation beim Mann. *Klin Wochenschr, 19:* 1231, 1940.

211. Sulman, F. G.: *Hypothalamic Control of Lactation.* New York, Springer-Verlag, 1970.

212. Sulman, F. G., and Winnik, H. Z.: Hormonal effects of chlorpromazine. *Lancet, 1:* 161, 1956.

213. Talwalker, P. K., Ratner, A., and Meites, J.: In vitro inhibition of pituitary prolactin synthesis and release by hypothalamic extract. *Am J Physiol, 205:* 213, 1963.

214. Taubert, H. D., Haskins, A. L., and Moszkowski, E. F.: The influence of thioridazine upon urinary gonadotropin excretion. *South Med J, 59:* 1301, 1966.

215. Tenenblatt, S. S., and Spagno, A.: A controlled study of chlorpromazine therapy in chronic psychotic patients. *J Clin Psychopathol, 17:* 81, 1956.

216. Thomas, A., and Kudelski, C.: Galactorrhée chez une tabétique. *Rev Neurol (Paris), 2:* 665, 1932.

217. Thompson, J. P., and Kempers, R. D.: Amenorrhea and galactorrhea. *Am J Obstet Gynecol, 93:* 65, 1965.

218. Thompson, R. J., and Mellinger, R. C.: The effects of clomiphene citrate in patients with pituitary-gonadal disorders. *Am J Obstet Gynecol, 92:* 412, 1965.

219. Toaff, R., and Sadovsky, A.: Galactorrhea and amenorrhea in pituitary adenomata. *Harefuah, 41:* 191, 1951.

220. Turkington, R. W.: Ectopic production of prolactin. *N Engl J Med, 285:* 1455, 1971.

221. Turkington, R. W.: Measurement of prolactin activity in human serum by the induction of specific milk proteins in mammary gland *in vitro. J Clin Endocrinol Metab, 33:* 210, 1971.

222. Turkington, R. W.: Serum prolactin levels in patients with gynecomastia. *J Clin Endocrinol Metab, 34:* 62, 1972.

223. Turkington, R. W.: Secretion of prolactin by patients with pituitary and hypothalamic tumors. *J Clin Endocrinol Metab, 34:* 159, 1972.

224. Turkington, R. W.: Phenothiazine stimulation test for prolactin re-

serve: the syndrome of isolated prolactin deficiency. *J Clin Endocrinol Metab, 34:* 247, 1972.

225. Turkington, R. W.: Inhibition of prolactin secretion and successful therapy of the Forbes-Albright syndrome with L-dopa. *J Clin Endocrinol Metab, 34:* 306, 1972.

226. Turkington, R. W.: Prolactin secretion in patients treated with various drugs: phenothiazines, tricyclic antidepressants, reserpine, and methyldopa. *Arch Intern Med, 130:* 349, 1972.

227. Turkington, R. W., and MacIndoe, J. H.: Hyperprolactinemia in sarcoidosis. *Ann Intern Med, 76:* 545, 1972.

228. Turkington, R. W., Underwood, L. E., and Van Wyk, J. J.: Elevated serum prolactin levels after pituitary-stalk section in man. *N Engl J Med, 285:* 707, 1971.

229. Vaidya, R. A., Vaidya, A. B., Van Woert, M. H., and Kase, N. G.: Galactorrhea and Parkinson-like syndrome: an adverse effect of α-methyldopa. *Metabolism, 19:* 1068, 1970.

230. Van Wyk, J. J., and Grumbach, M. M.: Syndrome of precocious menstruation and galactorrhea in juvenile hypothyroidism: an example of hormonal overlap in pituitary feedback. *J Pediatr, 57:* 416, 1960.

231. Verbov, J. L.: Atopic dermatitis and persistent lactation. *Br J Dermatol, 79:* 726, 1967.

232. Vix, V. A.: Abnormal persistent lactation. *Minn Med, 44:* 188, 1961.

233. Volpé, R., Killinger, D., Bird, C., Clark, A. F., and Friesen, H.: Idiopathic galactorrhea and mild hypogonadism in a young adult male. *J Clin Endocrinol Metab, 35:* 684, 1972.

234. Walter, R.: Abnormal secretion from the mammary gland following removal of a dermoid and corpus luteum cyst of the ovary. *Mt Sinai J Med NY, 3:* 213, 1937.

235. Wanebo, H. J., and Rawson, R. W.: Lupus erythematosus complicated by the Chiari-Frommel syndrome and auto-immune thyroiditis. *Arch Intern Med, 124:* 619, 1969.

236. White, A. E.: Nonpuerperal lactation: a review with case reports. *Ann Intern Med, 52:* 1264, 1960.

237. Whitelaw, M. J., Benson, R. C., Kalman, C. F., and Crane, J. T.: Very early abortion in Ahumada-Del Castillo syndrome. *Am J Obstet Gynecol, 95:* 400, 1966.

238. Wider, J. A., Marshall, J. R., and Ross, G. T.: Familial galactorrhea in three sisters with oligo-ovulation. *JAMA, 209:* 669, 1969.

239. Wieland, R. G., Folk, R. L., Taylor, J. N., and Hamwi, G. J.: Studies of male hypogonadism. I. Androgen metabolism in a male with gynecomastia and galactorrhea. *J Clin Endocrinol Metab, 27:* 763, 1967.

240. Wieschhoff, H. A.: Artificial stimulation of lactation in primitive cultures. *Bull Hist Med, 8:* 1403, 1940,

241. Wilson, R. G., Singhal, V. K., Percy-Robb, I., Forrest, A. P. M., Cole, E. N., Boyns, A. R., and Griffiths, K.: Response of plasma prolactin and growth hormone to insulin hypoglycaemia. *Lancet, 2:* 1283, 1972.

242. Wolstenholme, G. E. W., and Knight, J.: Lactogenic Hormones (Ciba Foundation Symposium). Edinburgh, Churchill Livingstone, 1972.

243. Wolthuis, O. L., and de Jongh, S. E.: The prolactin production and release of a pituitary graft and of the hypophysis in situ. *Acta Endocrinol (Paris), 43:* 271, 1963.

244. Young, R. L., Bradley, E. M., Goldzieher, J. W., Myers, P. W., and Lecocq, F. R.: Spectrum of nonpuerperal galactorrhea: report of two cases evolving through the various syndromes. *J Clin Endocrinol Metab, 27:* 461, 1967.

245. Zondek, B., Bromberg, Y. M., and Rozin, S.: An anterior pituitary hyperhormonotrophic syndrome (excessive uterine bleeding, galactorrhoea, hyperthyroidism). *J Obstet Gynaecol Br Commonw, 58:* 525, 1951.

TABLE OF ABBREVIATIONS

ACTH   Adrenocorticotropic hormone
CNS   Central nervous system
FSH   Follicle-stimulating hormone
GH   Growth hormone
hGH   Human growth hormone
LH   Luteinizing hormone
LRH   LH-releasing hormone
MSH   Melanocyte-stimulating hormone
hPr   Human prolactin
oPr   Ovine prolactin
PIH   Prolactin-inhibiting hormone
PRH   Prolactin-releasing hormone
TRH   TSH-releasing hormone
TSH   Thyroid-stimulating hormone
SRIH   Somatotropin-release inhibiting hormone

AUTHOR INDEX

A

Adams, F., 85
Aguilar, R.F., 85
Ahumada, J.C., 27, 85
Albores Culebro, C., 10, 85
Albright, F., 88
Alivisatos, J.G., 93
Anderson, M.S., 85
Apostolakis, 11, 48
Arenas Adarve, M., 85
Argonz, J., 27, 85
Arimura, A., 93, 96
Aruffo, R.N., 85
Ashkar, P.A., 30, 60, 85
Assael, M., 91
Atkinson, F.R.B., 10, 38, 85
Audibert, A., 87
Aufses, A.H., 46, 85
Averill, R.L.W., 85
Ayd, F.J., Jr., 85

B

Bab, H., 38, 85
Baba, Y., 93
Baker, B.L., 88
Barbeau, A., 88
Barker, A., 85
Barker, M., 85
Barnes, A.C., 95
Bates, R.W., 10, 39, 86, 95
Batrino, M.L., 93
Batzdorf, U., 90
Bayliss, P.F.C., 85
Bearzi, V.L., 86
Bell, E.T., 93
Bellut, H., 86
Benjamin, F., 86
Benson, R.C., 98
Bentson, J.R., 90
Bercovici, B., 28, 39, 86
Bergenstal, D.M., 92

Berger, R.L., 46, 86
Besser, G.M., 88
Bird, C., 98
Bittorf, A., 10, 86
Bivin, G.D., 26, 86
Blank, N., 90
Block, M.B., 95
Blum, D.M., 86
Bøler, J., 88
Bolognese, R.J., 86
Bowers, C.Y., 86, 88, 96
Boyns, A.R., 99
Bradley, E.M., 99
Braga, C., 86
Braun, C., 86
Braverman, L.E., 86
Brazeau, P., 86
Brecher, E., 89
Bridson, W.E., 87
Briehl, W., 86
Briggs, 43
Bromberg, Y.M., 99
Brown, D.M., 42, 86
Brun del Re, R., 87
Bruno, O.D., 92
Buchberg, A.S., 89
Buckman, 52
Burgus, R., 86
Butcher, M., 86

C

Calliga, V., 93
Canfield, C.J., 10, 39, 86
Carlson, K.L., 97
Carmona, N., 89
Cartlidge, N.E.F., 86
Casper, D.J., 86
Charambach, A., 11, 87
Charco Entrena, F., 85
Chard, T., 86
Chiari, J.B.V.L., 29, 86

101

SUBJECT INDEX